W0293840

English Collocations in Use

How words work together for fluent and natural English

Self-study and classroom use

Michael McCarthy
Felicity O'Dell

CAMBRIDGE
UNIVERSITY PRESS

CAMBRIDGE UNIVERSITY PRESS
Cambridge, New York, Melbourne, Madrid, Cape Town, Singapore, São Paulo, Delhi

Cambridge University Press
The Edinburgh Building, Cambridge CB2 8RU, UK

www.cambridge.org
Information on this title: www.cambridge.org/9780521603782

© Cambridge University Press 2005

This publication is in copyright. Subject to statutory exception
and to the provisions of relevant collective licensing agreements,
no reproduction of any part may take place without the written
permission of Cambridge University Press.

First published 2005
5th printing 2007

Printed in Dubai by Oriental Press

A catalogue record for this publication is available from the British Library

ISBN 978-0-521-60378-2 paperback

Contents

Topics: Society and institutions

Basic concepts

Functions

Acknowledgements

The authors wish to thank their editors at Cambridge University Press, especially Martine Walsh and Nóirín Burke, whose vision, expertise, encouragement and persistent faith in the project has helped to make the book what it is. We also thank Alyson Maskell for the highly professional job she carried out in preparing the final manuscript for production and printing; without her eagle eye many slips and faults might have gone unnoticed. Linda Matthews, too, deserves our thanks for organising the production schedules for the book.

We must also thank the lexicography and computational team at Cambridge University Press who assisted us in preparing lists of collocations based on the Cambridge International Corpus, and especially Liz Walter, who also gave us invaluable advice based on her years of experience in compiling Cambridge dictionaries. We also thank Diane Nicholls for her valuable research and analysis of learner errors from the Cambridge Learner Corpus.

Also, as always, we thank our domestic partners for their patience and support during the writing of the book.

We have also received invaluable feedback from both teachers and students. Their comments have had a great influence on the final manuscript and we are very grateful to them. In particular we would like to thank the following teachers from all over the world who reviewed and piloted the material throughout its development:
Rosemary Hancock, Spain
Ales Klégr, Czech Republic
Gillian Lazar, UK
David Mathias, Thailand
Julie Moore, UK
Terry Nelson, South Korea
Malgorzata Szulczyńska

Produced by Kamae Design, Oxford
Illustrations by Nick Schon

To the student (and the teacher)

What is a collocation?

Collocation means a natural combination of words; it refers to the way English words are closely associated with each other. For example, *do* and *homework* go together, as do *make* and *mistakes*; *tall* goes with *man/woman* and *high* with *mountain*.

Why learn collocations?

You need to learn collocations because they will help you to speak and write English in a more natural and accurate way. People will probably understand what you mean if you talk about 'making your homework' or say 'My uncle is a very high man' but your language will sound unnatural and might perhaps confuse. Did you mean that your uncle is two metres tall or did you mean that he has a high position in government or business?

Learning collocations will also help you to increase your range of English vocabulary. For example, you'll find it easier to avoid words like *very* or *nice* or *beautiful* or *get* by choosing a word that fits the context better and has a more precise meaning. This is particularly useful if you are taking a written exam in English and want to make a good impression on the examiners.

How were the collocations in the book selected?

The collocations presented in this book were all selected from those identified as significant by the Cambridge International Corpus of written and spoken English and also the CANCODE corpus of spoken English, developed at the University of Nottingham in association with Cambridge University Press. The Cambridge International Corpus is a vast database of over 750 million words of real English taken from books, newspapers, advertising, letters and e-mails, websites, conversations and speeches, radio and television. By studying this corpus we obtained a representative picture of how English is really used and which words naturally and frequently go together. We also made much use of the Cambridge Learner Corpus, a corpus of learner English taken from tens of thousands of exam scripts from students taking Cambridge ESOL examinations all over the world. This particular corpus showed us what kind of collocation errors learners tend to make.

These corpora show that there are many thousands of collocations in English. So how could we select which ones would be most useful for you to work on in this book?

Firstly, of course, we wanted to choose ones that you might want to use in your own written and spoken English. So, in the unit on Eating and drinking we include, for example, *have a quick snack* and *processed food* but not *rancid butter* [butter that has gone bad], which is a very strong collocation, but one which has very limited use for most people.

Secondly, we decided it would be most useful for you if we focused on those collocations which are not immediately obvious and which the Cambridge Learner Corpus shows can cause problems for students. *A friendly girl*, *cold water* or *to eat an apple* are all collocations, but they are combinations which you can easily understand and produce yourself without any problems. So we deal here with less obvious – though equally useful – word combinations, with, for instance, *make friends* (not ~~get friends~~) and *heavy rain* (not ~~strong rain~~).

Idioms are a special type of collocation where a fixed group of words has a meaning that cannot be guessed by knowing the meaning of the individual words. We deal with them separately in *English Idioms in Use* and so do not focus on them here.

How is the book organised?

The book has 60 two-page units. The left-hand page presents the collocations that are focused on in the unit. You will usually find examples of collocations in typical contexts with, where appropriate, any special notes about their meaning and their usage. The right-hand page checks that you have understood the information on the left-hand page by giving you a series of exercises that practise the material just presented.

The units are organised into different sections. First we start with important information about collocations in general. Then there are sections looking at grammatical and other special aspects of collocations. The rest of the book deals with collocations that relate to particular topics such as *Weather* and *Business*, concepts such as *Time* or *Change* and functions such as *Agreeing and disagreeing* or *Liking and disliking*.

The book has a key to all the exercises and an index which lists all the collocations we deal with and indicates the units where they can be found.

How should I use this book?

We recommend that you work through the five introductory units first so that you become familiar with the nature of collocations and with how best to study them. After that, you may work on the units in any order that suits you.

What else do I need in order to work with this book?

You need a notebook or file in which you can write down the collocations that you study in this book as well as any others that you come across elsewhere.

You also need to have access to a good dictionary. We strongly recommend the *Cambridge Learner's Dictionary* or the *Cambridge Advanced Learner's Dictionary*, as both of these give exactly the kind of information that you need to have about collocations. They do this both through the examples provided for each word entry and through their special collocations boxes or mini-panels. For more information about Cambridge dictionaries and to do online searches you could go to dictionary.cambridge.org. Your teacher, however, may also be able to recommend other dictionaries that you will find useful.

So, a study of collocation is **highly recommended** (Unit 6) if you want to **make a good impression** (Unit 2) with your natural and accurate use of English. Above all, we hope that you will not only learn a lot but will also **have fun** (Unit 9) as you **do the exercises** (Unit 26) in this book.

1 What is a collocation?

A

A collocation is a pair or group of words that are often used together. These combinations sound natural to native speakers, but students of English have to make a special effort to learn them because they are often difficult to guess. Some combinations just sound 'wrong' to native speakers of English. For example, the adjective *fast* collocates with *cars*, but not with *a glance*.

We say …	*We don't say …*
fast cars **fast food**	~~quick~~ cars ~~quick~~ food
a quick glance **a quick meal**	a ~~fast~~ glance a ~~fast~~ meal

Learning collocations is an important part of learning the vocabulary of a language. Some collocations are fixed, or very strong, for example **take a photo**, where no word other than *take* collocates with *photo* to give the same meaning. Some collocations are more open, where several different words may be used to give a similar meaning, for example **keep to / stick to the rules**. Here are some more examples of collocations.

You must **make an effort** and study for your exams (NOT ~~do~~ an effort)
Did you **watch TV** last night? (NOT ~~look at~~ TV)
This car has a very **powerful engine**. It can do 200 km an hour. (NOT ~~strong~~ engine)
There are some **ancient monuments** nearby. (NOT ~~antique~~ monuments)

Sometimes, a pair of words may not be absolutely wrong, and people will understand what is meant, but it may not be the natural, normal collocation. If someone says *I did a few mistakes* they will be understood, but a fluent speaker of English would probably say **I made a few mistakes**.

B Compounds and idioms

Compounds are units of meaning formed with two or more words. Sometimes the words are written separately, sometimes they have a hyphen and sometimes they are written as one word. Usually the meaning of the compound can be guessed by knowing the meaning of the individual words. Some examples of compounds are **car park, post office, narrow-minded, shoelaces, teapot**.

It is not always easy to separate collocations and compounds and, where they are useful for learners or an important part of the vocabulary of a topic, we include some compounds in this book too.

Idioms are groups of words in a fixed order that have a meaning that cannot be guessed by knowing the meaning of the individual words. For example, **pass the buck** is an idiom meaning 'to pass responsibility for a problem to another person to avoid dealing with it oneself'. We deal with idioms in detail in the book *English Idioms in Use* in this series.

C Why learn collocations?

Learning collocations is a good idea because they can:

a) give you the most natural way to say something: *smoking is* ***strictly forbidden*** is more natural than *smoking is strongly forbidden*.
b) give you alternative ways of saying something, which may be more colourful/expressive or more precise: instead of repeating *It was* ***very*** *cold and* ***very*** *dark*, we can say *It was* ***bitterly*** *cold and* ***pitch*** *dark*.
c) improve your style in writing: instead of saying *poverty* ***causes crime***, you can say *poverty* ***breeds crime***; instead of saying *a* ***big meal*** you can say *a* ***substantial meal***. You may not need or want to use these in informal conversations, but in writing they can give your text more variety and make it read better: this book includes notes about formality wherever the collocations are especially formal or informal.

Exercises

1.1 **Read A and B and answer these questions.**

1 What is a collocation?
2 Which of these words does *fast* collocate with: *car*, *food*, *glance*, *meal*?
3 Which of these are compounds: *computer*, *narrow-minded*, *teapot*, *ancient monument*, *car park*?
4 What do we call expressions like *pass the buck* and *be over the moon*?

1.2 **Make ten collocations from the words in the box.**

an effort ancient bitterly make breakfast cold dark
engine forbidden mistakes have make meal monument
pitch powerful strictly substantial TV watch

1.3 **Are these statements about collocations true or false?**

1 Learning collocations will make your English sound more natural.
2 Learning collocations will help you to express yourself in a variety of ways.
3 Learning collocations will help you to write better English.
4 Using collocations properly will get you better marks in exams.
5 You will not be understood unless you use collocations properly.

1.4 **Put the expressions from the box into the correct category in the table below.**

make a mistake a storm in a tea cup live music checkpoint key ring
pull somebody's leg heavy snow valid passport teapot bitterly disappointed

compound	*collocation*	*idiom*

1.5 **Underline the collocations in this text.**

When I left university I made a decision to take up a profession in which I could be creative. I could play the guitar, but I'd never written any songs. Nonetheless I decided to become a singer-songwriter. I made some recordings but I had a rather heavy cold so they didn't sound good. I made some more, and sent them to a record company and waited for them to reply.
So, while I was waiting to become famous, I got a job in a fast-food restaurant. That was five years ago. I'm still doing the same job.

2 Finding, recording and learning collocations

A Finding collocations

There are two main ways in which you can find collocations.

- You can train yourself to notice them whenever you read or listen to anything in English. Look at the collocations that are worth learning from this short text in English.

> After **giving** Mark **a lift** to the airport, Cathy **made her way** home. What an exciting **life** he **led**! At times Cathy felt **desperately jealous** of him. She **spent her time** doing little more than **taking care of** him and the children. Now her sister was **getting divorced** and would doubtless be **making demands on** her too. Cathy had promised to **give** her sister **a call** as soon as she got home but she decided to **run** herself **a bath** first. She had a **sharp pain** in her side and hoped that a hot bath might **ease the pain**.

TIP Get into the habit of making a note of any good collocations you come across in any English text you read.

- You can find them in any good learner's dictionary.

  For example, if you look up the word *sharp* you will find some of these collocations:

  a **sharp pain**
  a **sharp bend/turn**
  a **sharp contrast/difference/distinction**
  a **sharp rise/increase/drop**

TIP When you look up a new word make a point of noting it down in several different collocations.

B Recording collocations

The best way to record a collocation is in a phrase or a sentence showing how it is used. Highlight the collocation by underlining it or by using a highlighting pen.

For example: I don't <u>have access to</u> that kind of secret information.
Or: Jim gave me a very useful piece of advice.

C Learning collocations

Learning collocations is not so different from learning any vocabulary item. The key things are to:

- regularly revise what you want to learn
- practise using what you want to learn in contexts that are meaningful for you personally
- learn collocations in groups to help you fix them in your memory. You might group together collocations relating to the same topic. Or you might group collocations based on the same word, for example:

  I must **find a way** to help him.

  Can you **find your way** back to my house?

  I **learnt the hard way** that Jack can't be trusted.

  Please tell me if I'm **getting in your way**.

  You must **give way to** traffic from the left.

  I've **tried every possible way** to get him to change his mind.

Exercises

2.1 **Underline 11 collocations in this text.**

My friend Beth is desperately worried about her son at the moment. He wants to enrol on a course of some sort but just can't make a decision about what to study. I gave Beth a ring and we had a long chat about it last night. She said he'd like to study for a degree but is afraid he won't meet the requirements for university entry. Beth thinks he should do a course in Management because he'd like to set up his own business in the future. I agreed that that would be a wise choice.

2.2 **Match the beginning of each sentence on the left with its ending on the right.**

1 She's having	her duty.
2 She's taking	a lecture.
3 She's giving	a party.
4 She's making	an exam.
5 She's doing	good progress.

2.3 **Correct the eight collocation errors in this text. Use a dictionary to help you if necessary.**

In the morning I made some work in the garden, then I spent a rest for about an hour before going out to have some shopping in town. It was my sister's birthday and I wanted to do a special effort to cook a nice meal for her. I gave a look at a new Thai cookery book in the bookshop and decided to buy it. It has some totally easy recipes and I managed to do a good impression with my very first Thai meal. I think my sister utterly enjoyed her birthday.

2.4 **Look at this entry for the verb *lead* in the *Cambridge Advanced Learner's Dictionary*. What collocations could you learn from this entry? Underline or highlight them. Then write one new sentence for each of them.**

lead CONTROL E /liːd/ *verb* [I or T] (**led, led**) to control a group of people, a country, or a situation: *I think we've chosen the right person to lead the expedition.* ○ *I've asked Gemma to lead the discussion.* ○ *Who will be leading the inquiry into the accident?*
• **lead *sb* by the nose** INFORMAL to control someone and make them do exactly what you want them to do

See also **Unit 3, Using your dictionary.**

FOLLOW UP

Use a dictionary to find three or four other good collocations for each of these words:
desperately   pain   wise   run
Write the collocations you find in an appropriate way in your vocabulary notebook.

3 Using your dictionary

A good learner's dictionary will give you information on collocations. Sometimes the information is highlighted in some special way. In other cases, the examples used in the dictionary include the most common collocations.

In the *Cambridge Advanced Learner's Dictionary* (CALD), common and useful collocations are given in **bold type**. Look at the CALD entry for the word *pain* and note how useful collocations are highlighted in bold.

> **pain** (E) /peɪn/ *noun* [C or U] **1** a feeling of physical suffering caused by injury or illness: *Her symptoms included abdominal pain and vomiting.* ○ *Are you **in*** (= suffering from) *pain?* ○ *She was in **constant** pain.* ○ *These tablets should help to **ease** the pain.* ○ *I felt a **sharp** pain **in** my foot.* ○ *He's been suffering various **aches and** pains for years.* **2** emotional or mental suffering: *It's a film about the pains and pleasures of parenthood.* ○ *The parents are still in great pain **over** the death of their child.*
> • **a pain (in the neck)** INFORMAL someone or something that is very annoying: *That child is a **real** pain in the neck.*

CD-ROM versions of dictionaries are useful because you can usually search for a lot more information very quickly indeed. The CALD CD-ROM has a special button labelled Collocations in many entries. Clicking on this button gives you a list of collocations. Here are the verb collocations for *pain*. The dictionary also gives adjectives and nouns which are used with *pain*.

> Collocations | CALD2
>
> **Collocations**
>
> **pain**
>
> Verbs
> experience / feel / suffer pain
> *I experienced chest pains and dizziness.*
> alleviate / ease / lessen / relieve / soothe pain
> *A hot bath may help to relieve the pain.*
> cause / inflict pain
> *He deliberately inflicted pain on his pupils.*
> complain of pain
> *She came in complaining of stomach pains.*
> pain subsides
> *As the pain subsided, I began to relax.*
> be racked with pain
> *He is emaciated and racked with pain.*

A good dictionary will also tell you if a collocation is formal or informal. For example, CALD indicates that **to take somebody up on an offer** is an informal collocation (**accept an offer** would be a more formal alternative).

> **offer** (E) /ˈɒf.əʳ/ (US) /ˈɑː.fɚ/ *noun* [C] when someone asks you if you would like to have something or if you would like them to do something: *"If you like I can do some shopping for you." "That's a very kind offer."* ○ *I must say the offer **of** a weekend in Barcelona quite tempts me.* ○ INFORMAL *One day I'll **take** you **up on*** (= accept) *that offer.*

TIP When you buy a dictionary, make sure it gives good, clear information about collocations. When you look up words, if you don't know the collocations, highlight them in your dictionary or transfer them to your vocabulary notebook.

Exercises

3.1 Answer these questions about collocations and dictionaries.

1 How does the *Cambridge Advanced Learner's Dictionary* show collocations?
2 So, which five collocations with *pain* can you see in the top box on the opposite page?
3 Why is a CD-Rom dictionary particularly useful?
4 What happens if you click on the Collocations button when using the *Cambridge Advanced Learner's Dictionary* CD-Rom?
5 How does the *Cambridge Advanced Learner's Dictionary* indicate that a collocation is informal?
6 Look at the dictionary that you normally use. Does it indicate collocations? If so how?
7 Look up *pain* in your own dictionary. Which of the collocations on the left-hand page does it either highlight or illustrate in example sentences?
Does it show any other interesting collocations for *pain*?
8 Look up the noun *offer* in your own dictionary. What collocations can you find?
Does the dictionary indicate whether the collocations are formal/informal? If so, how?

3.2 Put the expressions from the box into the correct category in the table below.

to suffer pain   to alleviate pain   to be racked with pain   to cause pain
to complain of pain   to ease pain   to experience pain   to feel pain
to inflict pain   to lessen pain   to relieve pain   to soothe pain   pain subsides

making others experience pain	*the experience of being in pain*	*making pain go away*

3.3 Look in a good learner's dictionary. What collocations do you find there for the word *ache*?

FOLLOW UP

Look up two or three words that you have recently learnt, using a good learner's dictionary. Write down any interesting collocations that are shown for those words.

4 Types of collocation

There are many different types of collocations. Here are some examples.

A Adjectives and nouns

Notice adjectives that are typically used with particular nouns.

Jean always wears red or yellow or some other **bright colour**.
We had a **brief chat** about the exams but didn't have time to discuss them properly.
Unemployment is a **major problem** for the government at the moment.
Improving the health service is another **key issue** for government.

B Nouns and verbs

Notice how nouns and verbs often go together. The examples below are all to do with economics and business.

The **economy boomed** in the 1990s. [the economy was very strong]
The company has **grown** and now employs 50 more people than last year.
The company has **expanded** and now has branches in most major cities.
The two **companies merged** in 2003 and now form one very large corporation.
The company **launched the product** in 2002. [introduced the product]
The price increase **poses a problem** for us. [is a problem]
The Internet has **created opportunities** for our business. [brought new opportunities]

C Noun + noun

There are a lot of collocations with the pattern *a ... of ...* .

As Sam read the lies about him, he felt **a surge of anger**. [literary: a sudden angry feeling]
Every parent feels **a sense of pride** when their child does well or wins something.
I felt **a pang of nostalgia** when I saw the old photos of the village where I grew up.

D Verbs and expressions with prepositions

Some verbs collocate with particular prepositional expressions.

As Jack went on stage to receive his gold medal for the judo competition you could see his parents **swelling with pride**. [looking extremely proud]
I was **filled with horror** when I read the newspaper report of the explosion.
When she spilt juice on her new skirt the little girl **burst into tears**. [suddenly started crying]

E Verbs and adverbs

Some verbs have particular adverbs which regularly collocate with them.

She **pulled steadily** on the rope and helped him to safety. [pulled firmly and evenly]
He **placed** the beautiful vase **gently** on the window ledge.
'I love you and want to marry you,' Derek **whispered softly** to Marsha.
She **smiled proudly** as she looked at the photos of her new grandson.

F Adverbs and adjectives

Adjectives often have particular adverbs which regularly collocate with them.

They are **happily married**.
I am **fully aware** that there are serious problems. [I know well]
Harry was **blissfully unaware** that he was in danger. [Harry had no idea at all, often used about something unpleasant]

Exercises

4.1 Complete each sentence with a collocation from A.

1 Come to my office ten minutes before the meeting so we can have ...
2 With her lovely dark hair Uma looks best when she wears ...
3 In your essay on the influence of TV, don't forget to discuss these ...
4 There is some crime in our town but it isn't ...

4.2 Replace the underlined words with a collocating verb from B.

1 We are going to <u>introduce</u> an exciting new product in June.
2 The economy <u>was extremely high</u> 20 years ago.
3 The new university they are planning will <u>provide</u> a lot of job opportunities.
4 There are always some problems when two companies <u>join together</u> but I think it will be worth it in the long run.
5 The increase in oil prices certainly <u>creates</u> a problem for us.
6 The company <u>got bigger</u> and has now added children's clothing to its product range.

4.3 Choose the correct feeling from the box to complete each sentence.

anger	horror	tears	nostalgia	pride	pride

1 Most older people feel a slight pang of .... as they think back on their schooldays.
2 Carla's father was filled with .... when he saw that she had dyed her beautiful black hair blonde.
3 When Paul saw how harshly the poor were treated by the wealthy landowners he felt a surge of ....
4 Swelling with ...., Dan watched his daughter pick up her violin and play.
5 When she saw her exam results, Kate burst into ....
6 If people have a sense of .... in their town, they are more likely to behave well there.

4.4 Look at E and F and choose the correct adverb to complete these sentences.

1 Perhaps it's a good thing that Ken's .... unaware of what people really think of him.
2 I am .... aware that there will be problems whatever we decide.
3 Nadya smiled .... as she watched the children playing happily in the garden.
4 My grandparents have been .... married for 45 years.
5 Place the glasses .... in the box – they're very fragile.
6 Paul whispered .... in Anna's ear that he would always love her.

4.5 Which of the sections A–F on the opposite page would each of these collocations fit into?

1 make a decision
2 blissfully happy
3 tread carefully
4 a surge of emotion
5 acutely embarrassing
6 roar with laughter
7 a key factor
8 prices rise
9 a ginger cat
10 burst into song

FOLLOW UP Make a page in your vocabulary notebook for each of the types of collocations listed on the opposite page.

5 Register

Often, collocations rather than individual words suggest a particular register. For example, phrases using *pretty* meaning *fairly* sound informal when used with negative adjectives (**pretty awful**, **pretty dreadful**, **pretty dull**), and are typical of spoken English.

A Spoken English

Here are some more collocations which are almost exclusively found in spoken English.

[1]extremely bored

[2]give me a phone call

B Formal English

Some collocations are typical of formal English and are most likely to be found in an official, often legal, context, such as in notices.

Passengers must not **alight from the bus** whilst it is in motion.

[get off the bus]

Cyclists must dismount here

[get off their bicycles]

Trespassers will be prosecuted

[people who go onto someone's land or enter their building without permission will be taken to court]

Please **dispose of**[1] **unwanted items** in the **receptacle**[2] **provided**

[1]throw away
[2]container used for storing or putting objects in

C Newspaper English

Some collocations – particularly ones that use short, dramatic words – are found mainly in newspapers. In most cases they would not normally be used in everyday conversation.

COMPUTER FACTORY TO **AXE JOBS**

[make staff redundant]

AIRLINE **SLASHES PRICES**

[cuts prices drastically]

GOVERNMENT **SPENDING** WILL **ROCKET** THIS YEAR

POLICE CRACK DOWN ON SPEEDING

[start dealing with it in a more severe way]

POLICE QUIZ 16-YEAR-OLD IN MURDER ENQUIRY

[ask questions]

FLU **OUTBREAK HITS** SOUTHERN EUROPE

D Business English

Some collocations are characteristic of business English.

to **submit a tender** [present a document offering to do a job and stating the price]
to **raise capital** [get money to put into a business]
to **go into partnership with** someone [agree to start or run a business with someone]
to **start up a business**

Exercises

5.1 **Underline formal (F) or informal (I) collocations in these sentences (one per sentence) and put F or I in the brackets at the end.**

1 Cyclists should dismount before crossing the footbridge. ( )
2 Never dispose of batteries and similar items by throwing them onto a fire. ( )
3 The students were all bored stiff by the lecture. ( )
4 Passengers must alight from the bus through the rear door. ( )
5 The grass badly needs cutting. ( )
6 Please place all used tickets in the receptacle provided as you leave the building. ( )

5.2 **Underline typical news/media collocations in these newspaper clips.**

1
OIL COMPANIES SLASH PRICES
There was good news for motorists today as pump prices were lowered by the major oil companies.

2
DETECTIVES QUIZ BUSINESSMAN OVER MISSING TEENAGER
Senior detectives interviewed a man who has been named as prime suspect in the case of a missing 18 year-old who is feared to have been abducted.

3
FLOODS HIT CENTRAL REGION
Towns and villages in the Central region were battling against floods tonight as heavy rain continued.

4
CAR FIRM TO AXE 200 JOBS
The Presco car firm has announced that 200 workers will be made redundant at its Kenton factory. The job losses are the result of falling profits.

5.3 **Rewrite the headlines in exercise 5.2 using collocations more typical of ordinary conversation, as if you were telling a friend the news. Start each answer with 'Have you heard...?' Use a dictionary if necessary.**

5.4 **Match the beginning of each sentence on the left with its ending on the right to make typical collocations used in business English.**

1 We raised	partnership to develop a new range of products.
2 They submitted	capital to expand the business.
3 They went into	a business to supply sports equipment to schools.
4 We started up	a tender for the new stadium.

5.5 **Choose a formal or informal collocation as instructed at the end of each sentence. Use a dictionary if necessary.**

1 She was *dead / extremely* keen to meet the new director. (informal)
2 We should be *boarding the aircraft / getting on the plane* in about ten minutes. (formal)
3 Mr Trotter *paid for / bore the cost of* the repairs. (formal)
4 I *withdrew from / dropped out of* my university course after a year. (informal)
5 The president *launched into / embarked upon* a detailed explanation of his policies. (informal)

6 Intensifying adverbs

In English there are lots of other ways of saying *very* or *very much*. For example, we can use words such as *highly*, *utterly*, *bitterly*, *deeply*. These alternatives collocate strongly with specific words, and other combinations often sound unnatural.

A *Highly*

collocations	*comments*
(un)likely unusual successful competitive profitable effective controversial recommended	*Highly* is used with some probability words (*likely, unusual*). With the exception of **highly controversial** it usually combines with very positive words. **Extremely** can also be used with all the opposite adjectives except *recommended*.

It is **highly unlikely** that I'll finish my work on time.
Jill's **highly unusual** behaviour began to worry her parents.

B *Absolutely, utterly*

collocations	*comments*
ridiculous stupid impossible wrong alone appalled convinced devastated miserable	*Absolutely* and (slightly more formal) *utterly* combine with adjectives with very extreme meanings where we can't use *very*. For example, we say **absolutely/utterly exhausted**, not ~~*very*~~ *exhausted*, whereas we say *very tired*, but not ~~*absolutely*~~ or ~~*utterly*~~ *tired*. Often, but not always, these words have negative connotations.

It was an **absolutely stupid** comment to make.
The whole area was **utterly devastated** after the earthquake.

C *Bitterly, deeply, ridiculously, strongly*

word	*collocations*	*comments*
bitterly	**disappointing/disappointed resent criticise regret complain cry weep**	carries a feeling of deep sadness; used slightly more in writing than in conversation
deeply	**ashamed concerned shocked committed moved affected hurt** (of feelings) **regret care religious unhappy**	collocates mainly with words associated with feelings; used slightly more in writing than in conversation
ridiculously	**cheap expensive easy low high long short small large early**	suggests something extreme, which seems unbelievable or unreasonable
strongly	**oppose influence believe deny recommend support condemn suggest feel argue object**	collocates with verbs, particularly verbs that relate to having an opinion

I was **bitterly disappointed** when I failed the exam.
Professor McDellvit was always **deeply committed** to her students.
The restaurant was **ridiculously expensive**. I don't think we'll go there again.
I would **strongly recommend** that you learn a foreign language.

Exercises

6.1 **Choose an adverb from the box to replace *very* in each of these expressions.**

utterly strongly bitterly ridiculously highly deeply

1 very ashamed
2 very cheap
3 very controversial
4 very stupid
5 very successful
6 very disappointing
7 very opposed
8 very ridiculous
9 very easy
10 very concerned

6.2 **Use a collocation from exercise 6.1 to complete each of these sentences.**

1 The flight from London to Rome was .... It only cost 20 euros.
2 Some people love her new book, others are very angry about it. It is ....
3 His father was a pacifist all his life and was .... to war.
4 The exam results were .... for the whole class. We had all expected to do much better.
5 When I realised how much my selfish behaviour had upset everyone, I was ....
6 In the 1990s she ran a(n) .... company which made outstanding profits.
7 Everyone got more than 95% correct in the test; it was ....
8 You must apologise immediately. It was a(n) .... remark to make.
9 She has always been .... about the environment and would like to work for a conservation agency.
10 That you should even *think* that I would steal money from you is ....! You must be crazy!

6.3 **In each of these sets of phrases, one is not a correct collocation. Cross out the incorrect one.**

1 strongly recommend strongly influence strongly love strongly dislike
2 highly educated highly profitable highly unusual highly exhausted
3 bitterly regard bitterly regret bitterly resent bitterly criticise
4 absolutely convinced absolutely tired absolutely devastated absolutely absurd
5 deeply unhappy deeply religious deeply successful deeply committed

6.4 **In this short text, the writer has often misused the word *strongly*. Correct the wrong collocations using adverbs from the box. Use each adverb once only.**

bitterly strictly deeply utterly

Everyone was complaining strongly when they heard about the new plan. People were strongly shocked to hear that children would be strongly forbidden to use the sports ground and most people were strongly opposed to the new rules. Even people who normally never expressed an opinion were strongly appalled by the proposals.

7 Everyday verbs 1

This unit deals with *make* and *do*, two verbs that many learners have problems with. If you remember that the basic meaning of *make* is about producing something and the basic meaning of *do* is about performing an action, then the collocations on this page may seem more logical.

A *Make*

collocation	*example*
make arrangements for	The school can **make arrangements for** pupils with special needs.
make a change / changes	The new manager is planning to **make some changes**.
make a choice	Jill had to **make a choice** between her career and her family.
make a comment / comments	Would anyone like to **make any comments** on the talk?
make a contribution to	She **made a** useful **contribution to** the discussion.
make a decision	I'm glad it's you who has to **make the decision**, not me.
make an effort	Joe is really **making an effort** with his maths this term.
make an excuse	I'm too tired to go out tonight. Let's **make an excuse** and stay at home.
make friends	Karen is very good at **making friends**.
make an improvement	Repainting the room has really **made an improvement**.
make a mistake	They've **made a mistake** in our bill.
make a phone call	I've got to **make some phone calls** before dinner.
make progress	Harriet is **making progress** with all her schoolwork.

B *Do*

collocation	*example*
do your best	All that matters in the exam is to **do your best**.
do damage	The storm **did some damage** to our roof.
do an experiment	We are **doing an experiment** to test how the metal reacts with water.
do exercises	We'll **do some exercises** practising these collocations tomorrow.
do someone a good turn / do someone a favour	Scouts and guides are supposed to **do someone a good turn** every day.
do harm	Changing the rules may **do** more **harm** than good.
do your hair	No, I'm not ready. I haven't **done my hair** yet.
do your homework	My son has to **do his homework** straight after school.
do the ironing/shopping/ washing, etc.	I'll **do the washing** if you **do the ironing**.
do some work	We'll **do some work** on our project and then we'll go to the cinema.

TIP Notice all the patterns that you can see in these tables. For example, *make a comment*, *make an excuse* and *make a contribution to a discussion* are all connected with saying things. Noticing connections like this may help you to remember the correct collocation.

Exercises

7.1 **Use a collocation with *make* and a noun instead of the underlined words in each of these conversations.**

1 Miriam: The bill says we've had three desserts. We only had two.
Rosa: The waiter must have been mistaken.

2 Kim: It's so difficult. Should I take the job or not?
Todd: I know it's difficult. But you have to decide one way or the other.

3 Jane: Can you and Brian come to dinner on Saturday?
Jill: Yes, we'll have to arrange to get a babysitter, but it should be OK.

4 Brona: Did you hear about the air traffic controllers' strike in the USA?
Aaron: Yes. We had to change our travel itinerary because of it.

5 Pete: Can I have chips *and* rice with my lunch?
Clare: No, you have to choose, chips or rice, but not both.

6 Fran: Do you intend to speak at the meeting?
Gloria: Yes, I hope I can contribute to the debate.

7.2 **Choose the correct collocation, *do* or *make*.**

1 Did the fire *do / make* much damage to the factory?
2 I hate *doing / making* my homework at the last minute.
3 You must *do / make* an effort to work harder.
4 Did you *do / make* any work at the weekend?
5 We are trying to *do / make* improvements to the system for registering.
6 Do you think it would *do / make* any harm if I cut some leaves off this plant?

7.3 **You are designing a questionnaire for your school magazine. Complete each question with *do* or *make*.**

How NICE are you?	ALWAYS	SOMETIMES	NEVER
1 Do you always .... your best to be on time when meeting a friend?	☐	☐	☐
2 Do you ever .... the cooking at home?	☐	☐	☐
3 Do you .... excuses if someone asks you to .... a big favour for them?	☐	☐	☐
4 Do you ever .... negative comments about your friends' hair, clothes, etc?	☐	☐	☐
5 Do you find it easy to .... friends?	☐	☐	☐

Give yourself three points for 'always', two for 'sometimes', one for 'never'. Turn the page to find out how nice you really are.

8 Everyday verbs 2

Get is a very common verb in English, but it is not always appropriate for talking about changes. Note also alternatives to *get* which can improve your style.

A *Go*, not *get*

Go is used for changes in people's personality, appearance and physical abilities:
People **go mad/bald/grey/blind/deaf**.

Go is often used for sudden, usually negative, changes:
He was very embarrassed and his face **went red**.
Suddenly the sky **went** very **dark** and it started to rain.

Go can also be used for slower colour changes:
The pages of the book had **gone yellow** over the years.

B *Turn*, not *get*

Turn often collocates with colours:
The sky **turned gold** as the sun set.
When the tomatoes **turn red**, the farmers pick them and sell them.
The news gave his mother such a shock that her hair **turned white** overnight.

C *Get* and *become*

Get and *become* can often be used with the same collocations, but *become* is more formal and is therefore more appropriate in essays:
She gave up smoking when she **became pregnant**.
I would like to **become involved** in raising money for charity.

The same is true for collocations with adjectives such as *angry*, *bored*, *excited*, *depressed*, *upset*, *impatient*, *violent*:
He **became depressed** after his wife's death.

Become, not *get*, is used with the following: *extinct*, *(un)popular*, *homeless*, *famous*.
Our local baker's has **become famous** for its apple tarts.

D Alternatives to *get* and *become*

She **fell ill** and was taken to hospital.
Everyone **fell silent** when they heard the shocking news.
As my father **grew older**, he spent less time working.
The noise **grew louder** and soon we realised it was a plane approaching.

E Overusing and misusing *get*

Here are some sentences from students' essays where *get* is wrongly used.

sentences with **get**	*more appropriate alternatives*
I was able to get new friends.	I was able to **make** new **friends**.
A year ago he got a heart attack.	A year ago he **had/suffered a heart attack**.
If I get a child of my own one day ...	If I **have a child** of my own one day ...
I was getting crazy.	I was **going crazy**.
In June, I got a baby, James.	In June, I **had a baby**, James.

Exercises

8.1 Answer these questions using collocations from A and B.

1 What can happen to men as they get older? (Clue: Think of their hair.)
2 What can happen if you are embarrassed? (Clue: Think of your face.)
3 What can happen if you get bad news? (Clue: Think of your face or hair.)
4 What can happen to the pages of a newspaper after a long time?
5 What happens to strawberries as they ripen?
6 The poet John Milton lost his eyesight at the end of his life. What is another way of saying that?
7 The composer Beethoven lost his hearing at the end of his life. What is another way of saying that?
8 At the end of Shakespeare's play, Hamlet loses his mind. What is another way of saying that?
9 If it is about to rain, what might happen to the sky?

8.2 Look at C, D and E opposite. Correct these sentences.

1 Dinosaurs got extinct thousands of years ago.
2 When I get married, I'd like to get lots of children.
3 Janet fell depressed after failing her final exams.
4 Hamid has always dreamt of getting famous.
5 Would you be interested in growing involved in this project?
6 More people have got homeless this year than in any previous year.
7 My sister got a baby last week.
8 My grandfather got a heart attack last winter.

8.3 Replace each use of *get* with a verb from the box.

become	fall	become	grow	have	make

As you get older, you'll begin to understand your parents better. Getting angry with them all the time doesn't help. You may not want to go to summer camp when none of your friends will be there, but your parents know you will soon get new friends there. You would all have gone on a family holiday together if your grandmother hadn't got ill, but surely you can understand why they don't want to leave her. You'll feel much more sympathetic to your parents' feelings when you get a child of your own!

8.4 Complete the collocations in these sentences.

1 I think I'd go .... if I had to put up with such a terrible boss!
2 It was a wonderful sunset. The sky .... gold and we sat on the terrace enjoying it.
3 Once upon a time the walls were probably cream but they have .... brown now and badly need repainting.
4 When I start .... grey, I'm definitely going to dye my hair.
5 As the headmaster walked into the hall, the children all .... silent.
6 The noise on the street .... louder and I looked out of the window to see what was happening.
7 My grandmother is a little afraid of .... ill while she is abroad.
8 I was so embarrassed that I .... bright red.

9 Everyday verbs 3

A *Have*

Note that these verbs collocate with *have* rather than any other verb (e.g. *get* or *make*).

collocation	*example*
have an accident	Mr Grey **had an accident** last night but he's OK now.
have an argument / a row	We **had an argument / a row** about how to fix the car.
have a break	Let's **have a break** when you finish this exercise.
have a conversation/chat	I hope we'll have time to **have a chat** after the meeting.
have difficulty	The class **had difficulty** understanding what to do.
have a dream/nightmare	I **had a nightmare** last night.
have an experience	I **had a** frightening **experience** the other day.
have a feeling	I **have a feeling** that something is wrong.
have fun / a good time	I'm sure you'll **have fun** on the school trip.
have a look	The teacher wanted to **have a look** at what we were doing.
have a party	Let's **have a party** at the end of term.
have a problem / problems	Ask the teacher if you **have problems** with the exercise.
have a try/go	I'll explain what to do and then you can **have a go/try**.

B *Take*

Hi, Jean,

We're so glad we decided to **take a holiday** here. Yesterday we **took a trip** to the mountains. First we **took a train** to a little town and then we **took a bus** going to various villages and got off when we saw one that we **took a liking to**. Of course, we were **taking a risk** as we didn't know exactly what we'd find there. But we were lucky. Some kids **took an interest in** us and showed us some great places. We **took** a lot of **photos**.

Have you done anything yet about your job? I'd **take a chance** and leave if I were you. No point in staying somewhere where the boss has **taken a dislike to** you! **Take advantage of** being in London – there are always plenty of jobs there. You'll soon find something else, so **take action**, that's my advice! Good luck!

Ellen

C *Pay*

collocation	*example*
pay attention	You must **pay attention** to the teacher.
pay a compliment	I was trying to **pay** her **a compliment** but she misunderstood.
pay your (last) respects	At a funeral people **pay their last respects** to the person who has died.
pay tribute [formal]	When Jack retired, his boss made a speech **paying tribute** to all he had done for the company.

TIP There are other common verbs in English which have strong and possibly surprising collocations. Notice any that you find with, for example, *break*, *fall*, *run* and *take*.

Exercises

9.1 **Complete the questions using collocations from A opposite.**

1 You want a friend to look at a letter you have written before you send it.
YOU: Could you ....?
2 You want to know why your two friends aren't speaking to each other.
YOU: Why aren't you speaking to Rosa? Did you ....?
3 A friend comes to school on crutches with a bandage round her head.
YOU: What happened? Did you ....?
4 You want to know if a friend did lots of enjoyable things on their recent holiday.
YOU: How was the holiday? Did you ....?
5 You are having a meeting with some colleagues. You think it is time to stop for half an hour or so.
YOU: Shall we ....?
6 A friend has just bought a new bicycle. You'd like to ride it to see what it's like.
YOU: Nice bike! Can I ....?
7 You want to talk informally to your teacher about what to do next year.
YOU: When you're free, could I ....?
8 A friend is trying with difficulty to read your address, which you have just written down for them.
YOU: What's the matter? Are you ....?

9.2 **Choose the correct collocation.**

1 She *had / took / paid* attention to what I told her and started working harder.
2 I *had / made / took* over a hundred photographs on my trip to Antarctica.
3 She *made / paid / brought* me a nice compliment yesterday.
4 I *got / made / had* a bad dream last night and woke up sweating.
5 The President *made / gave / paid* tribute to all the people who had supported him.
6 I *got / took / had* a liking to our new teacher the moment I met her.
7 I *gave / made / had* a feeling I had met Richard before, but I couldn't remember where.
8 I went to Douglas Farnham's funeral to *give / take / pay* my last respects to a fine man.
9 I think I'll *take / make / do* a chance and leave my flight booking till the last minute. I may get a cheaper ticket.
10 Shall we *make / get / have* a party for Jane? She's leaving the school next week.
11 We need to *make / get / take* action immediately!
12 I *had / got / took* a feeling that he was trying to hide something from me.

9.3 **Which collocations in this text could be replaced by collocations with *take* instead of the verbs used?**

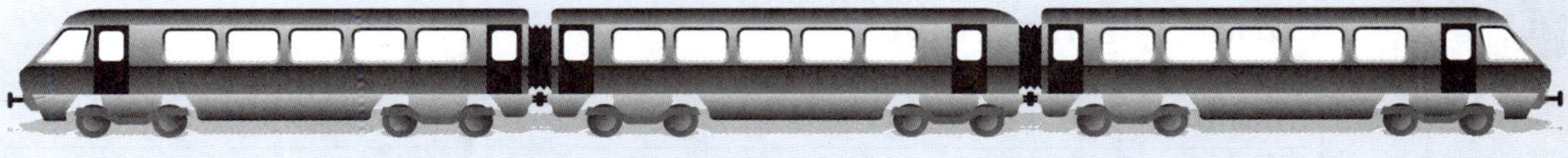

Next time you go on a trip to the coast, why not get the train?

Why suffer endless delays in long traffic jams? And why run risks when you're travelling – travel by train and arrive safely. What's more, if you decide to have a holiday in the capital city, you'll have a more relaxing time if you go by rail. Or why not pay a surprise visit to an old friend during an off-peak time? Call now and make use of our special offers.

0800 347655

10 Synonyms and confusable words 1

A Common synonym pairs

The (a) and (b) words in each pair in the table have similar meanings. Sometimes either word can be used in a sentence to give the same meaning, but in the collocations below only one word is possible.

synonyms	*(a) example*	*(b) example*
(a) close (b) shut	The chairperson **closed the meeting** at 4.30. [We **close meetings/discussions/ conferences**, etc.]	She was very rude. She said '**Shut your mouth!**' [impolite way of telling someone not to speak] A dentist might ask you to *close* your mouth. *Shut* is generally more informal.
(a) start (b) begin	It was a cold morning and I could not **start my car**. [*Start*, NOT ~~begin~~, is used for engines and vehicles.	Before the universe **began**, time and space did not exist. [*Begin* is preferred in more formal and abstract contexts.]
(a) big (b) large	It was a **big decision** to make. There were some **big problems** to solve.	I wanted the sweater in the **large size** but they only had medium.
(a) end (b) finish	The **film ended with** the hero dying. They **ended their relationship** a year ago. [*End* here means decide to stop.]	I haven't **finished my homework** yet. [*Finish* here means complete.]

B Groups of words with similar meanings

Words meaning 'old'

I met an **old friend** the other day. It's a very **old building**.
She studied **ancient history**. In **ancient times**, life was very hard.
This shop sells **antique furniture**. She collects **antique jewellery**. [old and valuable]
I helped an **elderly person** who was trying to cross the road. [*elderly* is more polite than *old*]

Words meaning 'with no one or nothing else or with nothing similar'

Donna is a **single parent**; it's difficult for her to work full time.
He lives in a very **lonely place/spot** up in the mountains.
At first I felt **desperately lonely** when I moved from London to the countryside.
I **live alone**, but I don't like **travelling alone**; it's nice to be with someone.
There was just one **solitary figure** on the otherwise deserted beach. [one person on their own]
She was the **sole survivor** of the crash. Everyone else died. [only survivor]
I am **an only child**; I sometimes wonder what it would be like to have a brother or sister.
This is a **unique occasion**, with three past Prime Ministers all together in one room.

C Other synonym pairs

synonyms	*(a) example*	*(b) example*
(a) charge (b) load	I need to **charge my phone**. [used for batteries, electrical items]	They **loaded the lorry** and drove away. [used for cargoes, lorries, vans, ships, etc. and for weapons]
(a) injure (b) damage	Three **injured people** were taken to hospital after the accident. [collocates with words to do with people]	The shop tried to sell me a **damaged sofa** but I noticed it just in time. [collocates with words for things]
(a) grow (b) raise	In the south the farmers **grow crops**. [collocates with crops, plants]	In the north the farmers mostly **raise cattle**. [collocates with animals, children]

Exercises

10.1 Choose the correct collocation.

1 The dentist told me to *shut / close* my mouth.
2 I didn't know what to do when I got into my car and couldn't *start / begin* the engine.
3 I want to buy a sweater for my dad. He needs one in a *big / large* size.
4 I haven't *finished / ended* my essay yet. I can't decide how to *finish / end* it.
5 At what time do you plan to *shut / close* the conference?
6 All societies develop their own stories about how the world *started / began*.
7 It's far too *big / large* a problem for you to solve on your own.
8 It's never easy to *finish / end* a relationship.

10.2 Look at B. Complete each phrase with a word meaning either 'old' or 'alone'.

1 a .... figure on the horizon
2 a shop selling .... furniture
3 to be an .... child
4 the .... survivor of the accident
5 to study .... history
6 to live ....
7 to feel desperately ....
8 to catch up with .... friends
9 support for .... parents
10 a home for .... people

10.3 Correct these sentences.

1 Were many people damaged in the earthquake?
2 Single parents growing children without a partner's support are entitled to financial help from the government.
3 My mobile isn't working. I need to load the battery.
4 She has a lot of beautiful elderly jewellery.
5 When we moved house, two men helped us to charge the van.
6 That's not news – it's antique history!
7 I don't know how to charge a gun, let alone fire one.
8 I've never been very successful at raising plants.

10.4 Which of the collocations on the opposite page do these pictures illustrate?

1

2

3

4

5

6

FOLLOW UP Look up *big* and *large* in a good learner's dictionary of English and see what other collocations it suggests for them.

11 Synonyms and confusable words 2

A Verbs connected with gaining, winning and achieving

Note these typical collocations connected with 'gaining' or 'achieving'.

verb	*collocates with*	*example*	*comments*
gain	power, control, access	The socialist party **gained control** of the National Assembly.	*Gain* is often used with abstract nouns relating to political authority.
gain [formal]	a reputation, publicity, recognition, an advantage	Her paintings **gained recognition** thanks to a major exhibition in New York.	*Gain* is often used with abstract nouns that suggest benefit to the 'gainer'.
win	an award, a prize, a medal, a match	He **won a medal** in the 2004 Olympic Games.	*Win* is often used in contexts associated with competition.
win	a battle, a war, an election	The conservative party **won the** 1994 General **Election**.	*Win* is often used in contexts associated with fighting.
earn	a salary, money	I **earn $2110** a month.	You **earn money** by working for it.
make	a profit, money	The company **made a profit** last year.	You can **make money** by investing etc., not just by working.
achieve	success, your goals, your aims	It's difficult to **achieve success** in international sport.	*Achieve* is used mainly with abstract nouns.
beat/ defeat	a team, an opponent	He **defeated his opponent** in the tennis final.	You **win a match** but **beat/defeat an opponent**. *Defeat* is more formal than *beat*.

B Other words that are often confused

You'll need to **take** warm **clothes** when you go to Alaska. (NOT ~~carry~~)

I always **carry** my **mobile phone** whenever I go out. (NOT ~~wear~~)

She was **wearing a hat**. (NOT ~~carrying~~)

He kindly offered to **carry** my **suitcase** for me.

She's **wearing a dress**. (NOT ~~using~~)

He's **using a laptop**.

ERROR WARNING

Notice how *spend* is used when talking about time and money.
We **spent three days** in the mountains. It was wonderful. (NOT ~~passed~~)
If you buy a big car you'll have to **spend more money** on petrol. (NOT ~~use~~)
Last night I **spent two hours** watching TV. (NOT ~~stayed~~)
I **spent an hour** looking for the keys before I found them in my bag. (NOT ~~passed~~)

Exercises

11.1 **Look at A. Use a verb from the box in the correct form to complete each collocation.**

achieve beat earn gain make win

1 I don't have ambitions to .... a lot of money, I just want to be happy in life.
2 Jack has already .... a very good reputation as a talented lawyer.
3 Kim has .... several prizes for her singing.
4 It is important to have goals even if you do not always .... them.
5 Chris .... a lot of money when he sold some old shares on the stock exchange.
6 In the tournament Hannah .... all her opponents and .... the gold medal.
7 Nowadays John .... a very good salary.
8 In the cycle race, Henrik .... an advantage when several of his opponents had punctures.

11.2 **Look at the picture and answer the questions.**

1 What is the woman wearing?
2 What is the woman carrying?
3 What is the woman using?
4 What is the man wearing?
5 What is the man carrying?
6 What is the man using?

11.3 **Correct the nine collocation errors in this paragraph.**

Last year I got a new job and started gaining a lot more money. I realised I could afford to use more money on my holiday than I usually do and decided to pass a month in Australia. I knew it would be hot there and so I wouldn't need to carry warm clothes with me. In fact, I used a t-shirt and jeans all the time I was there. I carried a hat all the time too, of course, to protect me from the sun. It was fantastic there. I passed a week sightseeing in Sydney and then stayed the rest of the time travelling round the country. I even did my lifelong ambition of stroking a koala.

11.4 **Change the underlined words so that each sentence has the opposite meaning.**

1 The Democratic Party lost the election.
2 The ruling power has lost control of the situation.
3 Our team was defeated in the match.
4 I spent a lot of money last month.
5 Our company made a loss last year.

11.5 **Complete these questions. Then answer them.**

1 Where did you .... your last holiday?
2 How much money did you .... last week?
3 What do you always .... with you when you go out?
4 Have you ever .... a trophy?
5 What aim would you particularly like to .... in life?

12 Metaphor

If someone uses a metaphor, they use a word in a way that is slightly different from its basic meaning. For example, the first meaning of *sunny* is connected with the weather, so we talk about a **sunny day**. However, *sunny* can also be used in expressions like a **sunny smile**, the **children's sunny faces** to mean happy; in these collocations *sunny* is used in a metaphorical way. Metaphors are more common in written than spoken English and often have the effect of sounding quite poetic.

A Light and dark

Light in English is associated with happiness. So a **face shines** with pleasure and **eyes shine** with excitement or delight. If someone's **face lights up** or their **eyes light up**, they show that they suddenly feel happy. If an **atmosphere lightens** or a **mood lightens**, it becomes more relaxed or cheerful than it was.

Darkness is associated with unhappiness and negative feelings. **Dark thoughts** are gloomy or sinister ones and **dark days** or **dark times** are unpleasant times to live through. If someone's **face darkens** or their **eyes darken** or someone's **expression darkens**, then we know that that person is unhappy, often because they are feeling angry.

B Water

collocation	*example*	*comment*
ideas flow, conversation flows	It was a very successful meeting. The **ideas flowed**.	*Flow* suggests that things progress easily, without effort.
a flood / floods of tears, tears streaming down someone's face	The little girl was **in floods of tears**. **Tears were streaming down her face**.	Both of these metaphors about tears suggest the girl is crying a lot.
people pour/stream somewhere	**People poured** out of the hall at the end of the lecture.	*Pour* and *stream* suggest lots of people moving smoothly.
people trickle	**People trickled** into the concert hall.	*Trickle* suggests a few people moving slowly.
a stream of visitors/ traffic	There was a **stream of traffic** outside our room all night.	*Stream* suggests continuous movement.

C Fire and heat

Words associated with fire and heat often suggest anger in English. A **heated debate,** a **heated discussion** or a **heated conversation** is one in which people disagree in an angry way with each other. If you say that someone has a **fiery temper**, you mean that they often get suddenly angry. The word *flare* means *show a bright light in the dark*. If you say **tempers flared**, you mean that people became angry with each other. Similarly **violence flares up** and **troubles flare up**. These all mean that problems which existed in the past suddenly become serious again.

However, not all metaphors relating to fire suggest anger. If you feel very embarrassed, your **cheeks burn with embarrassment**. A *blaze* is a very bright fire. We talk about a **blaze of glory** or a **blaze of publicity** meaning there is a lot of it and it is spectacular.

TIP When you are reading English, try to notice metaphorical uses of language. This will help you to see how familiar words can be used in extra, interesting ways.

Exercises

12.1 **Use a word from the box in the correct form to complete each collocation. Use each word once only.**

shine	dark	light up	sunny	lighten	darken

1 I could tell Maria was in a good mood by the .... smile on her face.
2 The little boy's eyes .... when he saw his daddy approaching.
3 Let's put some happy music on to .... the atmosphere. Everyone's too serious.
4 My grandparents lived through the .... days of civil war from 1936 to 1939.
5 The girl's eyes .... with excitement as she prepared for the party.
6 Mr Garnham's expression .... as he was told the terrible news.

12.2 **Read these remarks by different people, then answer the questions.**

Jason: I was in floods of tears. It was such a sad film.
Thomas: An hour before the match there was already a trickle of vehicles entering the car park.
Emma: I had a heated conversation with Helena the other day.
Paula: I didn't think there'd be much traffic today but there was a steady stream of vehicles on the main highway.
Rob: Tempers flared, I'm afraid, and mine was one of them.
Yvonne: Everyone was pouring out of the stadium as I drove past.

	name(s)
1 Who saw a lot of cars?	
2 Who got very angry indeed?	
3 Who saw a lot of people all at once?	
4 Who had a disagreement or argument?	
5 Who saw a small number of cars?	
6 Who cried over something?	

12.3 **Put these words in order to make sentences.**

1 with / cheeks / embarrassment / burning / were / My
2 city / up / has / in / capital / flared / the / Violence
3 flowed / The / during / discussion / ideas / the
4 divorce / was / footballer's / The / publicity / surrounded / famous / a / by / blaze / of

12.4 **Answer the questions.**

1 What is most likely to be fiery: (a) someone's intelligence (b) someone's temper?
2 Which is the most typical collocation: a blaze of (a) temper (b) glory (c) joy?
3 What is most likely to be heated: (a) discussions (b) cheeks (c) troubles?
4 What is most likely to flare up: (a) love (b) interest (c) violence?

12.5 **Use a dictionary to find collocations using these words in a metaphorical way.**

1 bright 2 warm 3 cold

13 Weather

A Talking about the weather

It's great here. Have had **unbroken sunshine**[1] ever since we arrived. We're having a wonderful time – though in the middle of the day it's just too **scorching hot**[2] to do anything but lie on the beach **soaking up the sunshine**[3]. This is the life!

Anna

[1] only sunshine, no clouds in the sky
[2] extremely hot
[3] enjoying the sunshine

It's been **pouring with rain** all day. In fact I've never seen such **torrential rain**[4]! It's **freezing cold** in the tent – we all got soaked to the skin[5]. Every half hour we look out of the tent hoping for **a break in the clouds**. In vain! We're going to a hotel next year!

It **rained heavily** all day yesterday but it's dry at the moment. There's **thick cloud**, though, and it certainly **looks like rain**[6]. Quite **a strong wind is blowing** too! Am glad we brought warm clothes!

[4] heavy rain [5] very wet [6] looks as if it is going to rain

B Weather conditions

collocation	*example*	*comment*
weather deteriorates [opposite: improves]	The **weather** is likely to **deteriorate** later on today.	*Deteriorate* is quite formal – the **weather is getting worse** is more informal.
thick/dense fog patches of fog/mist a blanket of fog [literary] fog/mist comes down [opposite: lifts]	There is **thick fog** on the motorway. There are **patches of fog** on the east coast but these should **lift** by midday.	*Patches of fog/mist* are small areas of fog/mist, whereas *a blanket of fog/mist* is thicker and more extensive.
strong sun [opposite: weak]	Avoid going on the beach at midday when the **sun is strongest**.	
heavy rain (NOT ~~strong~~ rain) driving rain	Road conditions are difficult because of the **driving rain**.	*driving rain* = rain falling fast and heavily
heavy/fresh/crisp/thick/ driving snow	The **snow** is lovely and **crisp** this morning.	*crisp snow* = snow that is fresh and hard
hard frost	There will be a **hard frost** tonight.	opposite of *a hard frost* = *a light frost* (NOT a ~~soft~~ frost)
high/strong/light/biting winds the wind picks up [opposite: dies down] the wind blows/whistles	The **wind** was **light** this morning but it's **picking up** now and will be very **strong** by the evening. The **wind was whistling** through the trees.	*biting winds* = very cold winds If the wind picks up, it gets stronger.

C Extreme weather

FREAK[1] STORMS DEVASTATE SW

Yesterday **freak weather conditions hit**[2] the south-west of England. **Gale-force winds**[3] **caused** a lot of **damage** to property. A number of **buildings were destroyed, roofs were torn off** and **fences were blown down**. Several rivers **burst their banks**[4].

[1] very unusual or unexpected
[2] struck, badly affected
[3] extremely strong winds
[4] rivers flooded

Exercises

13.1 **Look at A and B opposite and complete these weather collocations.**

1 crisp ....
2 patches of ....
3 strong ....
4 a biting ....
5 a hard ....
6 torrential ....
7 unbroken ....
8 a blanket of ....

13.2 **Look at A and B opposite. Change the underlined words so that each sentence has the opposite meaning.**

1 There was a light wind yesterday.
2 The wind picked up in the evening.
3 The weather is likely to improve tomorrow.
4 It was scorching hot here yesterday.
5 There may be some light rain later on today.
6 The mist came down at about midday.

13.3 **Replace the underlined words in this letter with collocations from the opposite page.**

I wish I'd worn a warmer jacket. There's a very cold wind. At least it's not raining heavily today. I got extremely wet yesterday. I wish I was sunbathing on a Mediterranean beach.

13.4 **Answer these questions about the collocations on the opposite page.**

1 What might make a river burst its banks?
2 What can you probably see if someone says, 'It looks like rain'?
3 What kind of wind is a freak wind?
4 Is it harder to drive if there's dense fog or if there are patches of fog?
5 What kind of weather conditions have you got if the rain is described as driving rain?
6 If we talk about severe weather conditions *hitting* or *striking* an area, what kind of image is created?
7 What, apart from wind, can blow or whistle?
8 Which of these verbs suggests most destruction and which least?
The storm *destroyed / damaged / devastated* the town.

13.5 **Look up these words in your dictionary. Note down two more collocations for each one.**

wind

rain

snow

FOLLOW UP

Either listen to the weather forecast on an English language TV or radio channel **or** go to the website www.bbc.co.uk/weather. (You can enter the name of your own country to get information about the weather there.)
Make a note of any other useful weather collocations that you find.

14 Travel

A Travel, journey, trip

Look at these e-mails and note the different collocations for *travel*, *journey* and *trip*.

Jane,
Have you made your **travel arrangements** for the sales conference yet? If you want a good **travel agent**, I can recommend Atlas World. They specialise in **business travel**. Their number is 2587996. They're very helpful.
Rickie

Hi Mel,
I'm finally here after an extremely **tiring journey**! The flight was three hours late, they lost my luggage, then there were no taxis at the airport. I hope my **return journey**[1] is better! I'm at the Hotel Rex, room 1305, tel: 987745. Give me a call.
Simon

[1] The opposite of **return journey** is **outward journey**.

Hi Karen,
I know next week is a **business trip**, but you must do some sightseeing too while you're here. I suggest we take a **day trip** to Canamuca on the Sunday. It's about two hours by car, and we can take a **boat trip** to the island in the middle of the lake and have lunch there. Looking forward to seeing you on Monday. **Safe journey**[2].
David

[2] said to someone who is about to make a journey

Janine,
I got some **travel brochures** with details of **camping trips**. Want to meet for lunch to look at them? One of them is in Chile, but it's a long **overnight journey** from the capital to get there, so maybe we should look nearer home? Nice to dream of holidays during work time!
Lorna

B Flights

These collocations are all rather formal ones connected with flying:

Palair offers excellent **in-flight entertainment**, with the latest films and music.
The **in-flight magazine** includes maps and information about major airports.
[announcement by a cabin attendant] Ladies and gentlemen, we'll shortly be landing at Dublin Airport. Please **fasten your seatbelts**.
The passenger **boarded the plane** on time, but it was delayed taking off and she missed her **connecting flight** in Amsterdam.
Domestic flights are often more expensive than international ones. [flights within a country]
Do you normally prefer a **window seat** or an **aisle seat** when you fly?
We managed to get a **charter**[1] **flight**; it was half the price of the **scheduled**[2] **flight**.

[1]flight on a plane rented for special use
[2]regular flight organised by the company which owns the plane

The weather en route is fine, and we anticipate a **smooth flight**[3] to Stockholm today.

[3]The opposite is a **bumpy flight**

C Accommodation

We stayed in a small, **family-run hotel**.
The Panorama is a rather **run-down hotel** in a back street near the city centre.
The Palace is a **luxury hotel** on the main square of Porto Alegre.
As a student, I can't afford to stay in **smart hotels**. I always have to look for **budget accommodation**. [very cheap]
I'd advise you to **make a reservation** before you go. The hotels near the beach are very popular and get **fully booked** during the summer.

Exercises

14.1 **Complete each sentence with *trip*, *travel* or *journey*.**

1 I'll get some .... brochures today and we can start planning our holiday.
2 John is away on a business .... all week.
3 It's a rather difficult overnight .... to the mountains but it's well worth it.
4 I prefer to arrange my holidays myself rather than use a .... agent.
5 On Saturday we went on a day .... to an interesting old castle.
6 Was it a tiring .... from Seoul to Los Angeles?
7 On summer weekends we often used to go on camping ....
8 Do you use a special firm to arrange business .... for your staff?
9 Do you make your own .... arrangements or does your secretary do it all?
10 I hope your flight is on time tomorrow. Safe ....! See you at the airport.

14.2 **Complete these sentences.**

1 We couldn't .... a reservation; all the hotels were .... booked.
2 As I've got long legs I usually ask for an .... seat on a long flight, but on the flight to New York I had a .... seat and I got a great view of Manhattan as we came in, even though I didn't have much leg-room.
3 We're only scheduled to have about half an hour in Dubai, so I hope we don't miss our .... flight.
4 They seem to have much better in-flight .... on that airline; they have the latest films and you can play video games.
5 Passengers must .... their seatbelts before take-off and landing.
6 Passengers with seats in rows one to 25 are now invited to .... the plane.
7 The Principality Hotel was rather ....-down and we were very disappointed.
8 You can spend a lot of money and stay in a .... hotel or you can look for budget ....

14.3 **Answer these questions about travel collocations.**

1 What is the opposite of a smooth flight?
2 Which of these two kinds of flight do most people prefer and why?
3 What do we call a flight which is not a *charter* flight?
4 What do airlines often provide for passengers to read?
5 What is the difference between *a business trip* and *business travel*?
6 What is the opposite of *outward journey*?
7 If a hotel is family-run, is it especially trying to attract families as guests?

14.4 **Write about 100 words describing a recent personal travel experience. Use the collocations from this unit.**

FOLLOW UP

Next time you fly, look at the signs at the airports you pass through, which are often in English as well as the local language(s). Find and make a note of three useful collocations.

15 Countryside

A Writing about the landscape

From my room I look out over the **surrounding countryside**. It's very different from the **familiar landscape** I see from the windows at home. At home it's a **gentle landscape**[1] with **open fields**[2]. Here it's a **bleak landscape** with **rocky mountains** in the distance.

1 a landscape with nothing extreme or threatening about it
2 fields uninterrupted by woods or houses

Yesterday we **followed a path** down to the lake. As we **turned a corner**, we **caught a glimpse of**[3] a kingfisher standing in the water. John tried to **take a picture**[4] of it but it **caught sight of** us and flew off. A little further on we **rounded a bend**[5] and St John's Abbey **came into view**. The Abbey **fell into ruin**[6] about three hundred years ago. Although it **lies in ruins**, it is **well worth seeing** as it stands in a **dramatic setting** on a **steep slope** beside a **fast-flowing river** with **mountains towering**[7] above it.

3 saw for a moment
4 take a photo
5 turned a corner
6 became a ruin
7 mountains rising dramatically

The cottage is in some wonderful **unspoilt countryside**[8] on the edge of a **dense forest**[9]. Unfortunately the trees **block the view** of the **snow-covered mountains**. It has a little garden with a stream at the end of it. The **stream winds**[10] through the forest. They wanted to build a timber factory here but the local people said that it would **destroy the countryside** and, fortunately, their campaign to **protect the environment** succeeded.

8 countryside that has not been changed by industry or modern buildings
9 thick forest
10 makes lots of bends, doesn't flow in a straight line

B The language of tourism

collocation	*example*
uninterrupted view	From most rooms there are **uninterrupted views** of the castle. [nothing blocks the views of the castle]
panoramic view	From the top floor restaurant diners have a **panoramic view** of the countryside. [view over a very wide area]
spectacular view	From the balcony there is a **spectacular view** of the mountains. [very dramatic view]
enjoy/admire a view	We stopped for a few minutes to **admire the view**.
breathtaking scenery	The area has some **breathtaking scenery** – mountains, cliffs, lakes. [extremely striking and beautiful views]
dominate the landscape	The castle **dominates the landscape** for miles around. [can be seen from a long way away]
beach stretches	A beautiful **beach stretches** for miles along the coast.
sandy beach	The hotel has its own **sandy beach**.
secluded beach	You'll love the **secluded beaches**. [without many people]
golden sands	You can wander for miles along the **golden sands**.
peaceful/tranquil countryside	You can quickly go from the hustle and bustle of the town to the **tranquil countryside**. [formal]

Exercises

15.1 **Look at A. Complete the collocations to fit these pictures.**

1  2  3 

1 Near the lake there is an old house that .... ruin about a hundred years ago. It stands in a lovely landscape, surrounded by .... fields.
2 We .... a footpath along the river for about three kilometres. In the distance there were snow-.................................. mountains.
3 We walked through a .... forest; it was very dark among the trees.

15.2 **Correct the underlined collocation errors in this paragraph.**

A chain of <u>snowy</u> mountains runs down the east of the country. The Wassa River, the country's biggest, <u>dances</u> slowly from the northern mountains to the sea. Even in summer it is a <u>sour</u> landscape, with its dark, <u>stony</u> mountains and its cold streams. But for me it is the <u>family</u> landscape of my childhood and I am happy that the government has decided to <u>guard</u> this environment. It is a dramatic <u>set</u> which is <u>a lot</u> worth visiting for anyone who likes <u>spectacle</u> views.

15.3 **Choose the correct collocation.**

1 We *made / took / put* a lot of photographs because it was such a beautiful day.
2 As I *returned / turned* the corner I *made / caught / took* a glimpse of the house through the trees.
3 A long *sanded / sandy* beach *reached / ran / stretched* for miles in front of us.
4 Unfortunately, the new hotel *blocks / jams / stops* the view of the castle.

15.4 **Complete this collocation web for *countryside*.**

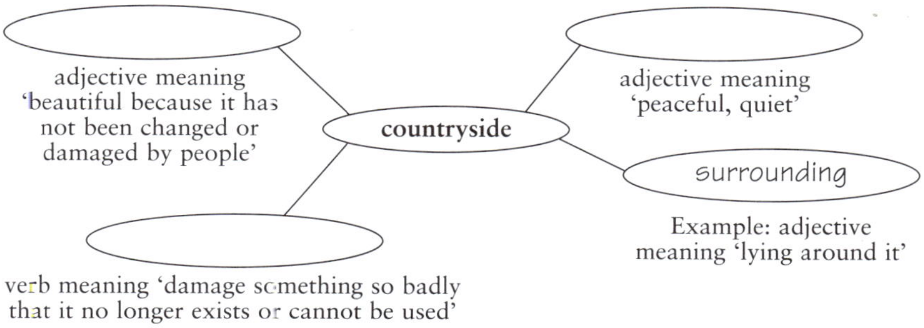

15.5 **Replace the words in brackets in each sentence with one word which collocates with the underlined word.**

1 It's a beautiful town and the <u>countryside</u> (which is all around it) is even more beautiful.
2 The tower (is the most important and visible thing on) <u>the landscape</u>. From the top of the tower, you get a <u>view</u> (which allows you to see a very wide stretch) of the surrounding area.
3 There are lovely <u>beaches</u> (with very few people on them).
4 We travelled through some <u>scenery</u> (which was extremely exciting and beautiful).
5 From the windows of our villa we had <u>views</u> (which were continuous, without any obstacles,) of the lakes and mountains.

16 Towns and cities

A Describing towns and cities for visitors

Look at these extracts from a magazine article about tourist cities.

The **city skyline** is a wonderful mix of old and new, and the city itself has a lot of busy, narrow **cobbled**[1] **streets**. The old town is a **conservation area** and it has a lot of **quaint**[2] **old buildings** dating back to the city's foundation in the 1500s.

1 made of a regular pattern of stones
2 attractive because of being unusual and especially old-fashioned

Doradella Street has a lot of **upmarket**[3] **shops** and rather **pricey**[4], sometimes **overpriced**, **restaurants**, but not far away is the Genasia district, where you'll find restaurants which offer **good value** and a more **relaxed atmosphere**.

3 for people with expensive tastes
4 expensive, in a negative sense

Royal Avenue runs from north to south, and is **lined with shops**. Behind it, the streets are full of **lively bars** and **fashionable clubs**. The **pavement cafés** and shops of Luna Square are pleasant but very expensive.

As you drive into the city, the **tree-lined avenues** of the **residential areas** are soon replaced by the **high-rise flats** of the **inner city**[5]. Then come the **imposing buildings** of the Parliament and government departments.

5 central part of a city where poorer people live and where there are often social problems

B Towns and cities and their problems

Here are some descriptions of the more negative aspects of towns and cities.

Some of the **inner-city areas** are an **urban wasteland**[1] and are somewhat dangerous for visitors. In fact some streets have become **no-go**[2] **areas**, with high crime. Many streets are **strewn with litter** and there are numerous **run-down**[3] **buildings**. There are some **deprived**[4] **areas** round the city centre with huge social problems. The **industrial zones** which lie on the edge of the city are grey and polluted.

1 a city area which is empty and in a bad condition
2 where the police and other authorities are afraid to enter
3 in very bad condition
4 not having the things that are necessary for a pleasant life, e.g. enough money, good living conditions

Triope is a **sprawling**[5] **city** with **bumper-to-bumper**[6] **traffic** all day long. The **exhaust fumes** can be a nightmare. The **volume of traffic** has increased in recent years and the **incessant roar**[7] of trucks and buses makes the city centre an extremely noisy place.
The **comfortable suburbs**[8] away from the city centre contrast sharply with the poor **shanty towns**[9] one sees on the way to the airport.

5 spread over a large area (slightly negative)
6 so many cars and so close that they are almost touching each other
7 very loud noise which never stops
8 a place from which many people travel in order to work in a bigger town or city
9 very poor houses made of discarded materials (e.g. tin, cardboard, plastic, etc.)

Exercises

16.1 **Which of the collocations in A opposite do these drawings illustrate?**

16.2 **Which of the collocations in the box have a positive meaning (+) and which have a negative meaning (–)?**

relaxed atmosphere lively bar over-priced restaurants urban wasteland no-go area
imposing building shanty town fashionable club run-down buildings

16.3 **Answer these questions using collocations from the opposite page.**

1 What might prevent you from sleeping in a house near a busy motorway?
2 Exhaust fumes will get worse if what increases?
3 What is the opposite of a restaurant which is good value?
4 What kind of area with poor, home-made houses could certainly be called a deprived area?
5 If an area is very interesting historically, what may it officially be called?
6 What is another way of saying an expensive restaurant?
7 What do we call blocks of flats which have many storeys, perhaps 20 or more?
8 What adjective could be used about an attractive and perhaps slightly unusual old building?

16.4 **Match the beginnings of each sentence on the left with its ending on the right.**

1 It is a sprawling	traffic all the way to the airport.
2 It is full of upmarket	runs from the castle to the river.
3 There was bumper-to-bumper	zones and some large supermarkets.
4 I get asthma from the terrible exhaust	with shops and cafés.
5 I live in a residential	city covering an enormous area.
6 Some of the more deprived	with litter.
7 The main street in town	area but work in the city centre.
8 The main street is lined	areas are not far from the city centre.
9 On the outskirts are some industrial	fumes in the city centre.
10 The streets were strewn	shops, which are too expensive for me.

FOLLOW UP Find a description in an encyclopaedia, tourist brochure or guide book of a city that you know well or are interested in. Make a note of any interesting collocations that you find there.

17 People: character and behaviour

A Your month of birth and your character

January You are **good company**[1] but you may have a **selfish streak**[2].

February You have **an outgoing personality** and a **good sense of humour**.

March You **have a vivid imagination**, but you tend to **lose your temper** too easily.

April You are **highly intelligent** with a **razor-sharp mind**.

May You **set high standards** for yourself and are **fiercely**[3] **loyal** to your friends.

June The best **aspect of your personality** is the way you always **put others first**.

July Although you can be **painfully shy** in social situations, at work you **give the impression of** being **supremely confident**.

August You **have a tendency** to make **snap decisions**[4].

September You have a strong **sense of responsibility** and always **keep your word**[5].

October You are good at **keeping secrets** and never **bear a grudge**[6].

November You find it hard to **keep your temper**[7] if you think someone is **making a fool out of you**[8].

December You can be **brutally honest**[9] and sometimes **hurt others' feelings**.

1 people enjoy being with you
2 you sometimes act in a selfish way
3 stronger than *extremely*
4 quick decisions
5 do what you say you will do, keep your promises
6 resent for a long time bad things others have done to you
7 not get angry
8 trying to deceive or trick you
9 honest in a way that may hurt

B Behaviour: verb + noun collocations

collocation	*example*	*comment*
play a joke/trick	The children **played a joke on** the teacher by hiding under their desks before she came into the room.	NOT ~~make~~ a joke/trick
take a joke	Fortunately, the teacher could **take a joke** and didn't punish them.	= didn't mind a joke being played on her
swallow your pride	Jane **swallowed her pride** and admitted that she was wrong.	= she did it even though it was embarrassing for her
throw a tantrum	The child **threw a tantrum** when I wouldn't buy him any sweets.	= behaved in a very uncontrolled manner
lose your patience	Finally I **lost my patience** and shouted at her.	= lost my temper, became angry
come to terms with	Nick has found it hard to **come to terms with** his illness.	= accept something psychologically
reveal your true character	Jack's failure to support her has certainly **revealed his true character**.	opposite = conceal/hide your true character

TIP Associating these collocations with people you know may help you to learn them.

Exercises

17.1 Which of the collocations in A describe negatives aspects of character?

17.2 Add the missing words in these letters to a magazine where readers are discussing their and others' characters. You are sometimes given the first letter.

1 I know that I .... a tendency to .... a grudge, but I just can't forget something bad a friend did to me recently. She has a selfish s.................... and doesn't care sometimes how much she .... my feelings. I am finding it increasingly hard to k.................... my temper with her. But perhaps it might be better to l.................... my temper and let her know how I really feel?
Silvia M.

2 I have always tried to .... others first and not to think of myself. I believe you should not lose your p.................... with your friends, but if someone seems to enjoy .... a fool out of you in front of other people, do those rules of friendship still apply?
Stefan P.

3 I'm a little shy, though not p.................... shy, but sometimes I think I .... the impression that I'm unfriendly. How can I convince people that I'm good c.................... and worth getting to know?
Tom W.

4 Should I talk about personal matters to my closest colleague at work? She is not very good at .... secrets and she has a very v.................... imagination. She always promises not to tell other people, but I'm not sure she always .... her word.
Jan H.

5 My boyfriend has a really friendly, o.................... personality and a great .... of humour. He's .... intelligent and has a ....-sharp mind. The perfect man. We've been together now for a year, and I like him a lot, but don't love him any more. Should I be b.................... honest with him and tell him?
Lydia T.

6 I think a friend is destroying himself with drugs. I feel a .... of responsibility towards him. He has always been f.................... loyal to me in good and bad times, which is a wonderful a.................... of his personality. I feel I ought to contact the police or social services, but I don't want to make a s.................... decision which I'll regret later.
Gary J.

17.3 Complete B's remarks in these conversations so that they mean more or less the same as A's, using collocations from the opposite page.

1 A: Bob's found it hard to accept psychologically the fact that he's now divorced.
B: Yes, he's found it hard .... with his new situation.

2 A: Kevin's problem is he can't laugh when people play jokes on him.
B: No, it's true. He just can't ...., can he?

3 A: Well, Sara's behaviour last night certainly showed the truth about her.
B: Yes, it certainly ....

4 A: She always has very high expectations of both herself and her children.
B: Yes, she always ....

5 A: Sam started screaming and stamping his feet when I tried to put him to bed.
B: Well, two-year-olds often ....

17.4 Look in your dictionary. Can you find any other collocations ...

1 ... where *word* has the meaning of promise?
2 ... where *temper* relates to behaviour?
3 ... where *sense of* ... relates to an aspect of character?

18 People: physical appearance

A Words describing people's physical appearance

Read these quotations taken from essays where students were asked to describe their family members.

My father has a **round face**, with **chubby**[1] **cheeks** and a **droopy**[2] **moustache**. My mother has a more **pointed face** and a **straight nose**. My younger sister is more like my father. She has an **oval**[3] **face** and an **upturned nose**. My older sister is like a model. She has a **slim figure** and a **slender**[4] **waist**. She has a **lovely complexion**[5] and beautiful **sleek**[6], **shoulder-length hair**, and she's always **immaculately groomed**[7]. I feel so ordinary next to her – I've got **coarse**[8] **hair** and rather **broad hips**, but she always says I look nice.

1 fat in a pleasant and attractive way
2 long and hanging down heavily
3 shaped like an egg
4 attractively slim (a rather formal, poetic word)
5 the natural colour and quality of a person's skin
6 smooth and shiny
7 her appearance is always tidy and looked after with great care
8 rough, and not smooth or soft

My father and my two older brothers are all **well-built**[9] with **broad shoulders**. My father is **going bald** but he still has a very **youthful appearance** for someone who is over forty. My brothers both have **thick hair** and **bushy**[10] **eyebrows**. My younger brother is only two – he's just a **tiny tot**[11], but he's very cute. My mother's side of the family mostly have **dark hair** – in fact my mother had **jet-black hair**[12] when she was younger, before she **went grey** – but on my father's side some have **fair hair** and some have **ginger**[13] **hair**.

9 have strong, attractive bodies
10 very thick
11 a small child
12 completely black
13 a red or orange-brown colour; used of people's hair

B More collocations describing appearance

A short, **dumpy woman** was selling flowers at a stall on the street corner. [short and quite fat woman; used more often of women than of men]

A **portly gentleman** answered the door. [fat and round; usually used of middle-aged and older men]

A **lanky youth** was standing at the street corner. [tall and thin and tending to move awkwardly]

I wouldn't like people to see me with **dishevelled hair** and dirty clothes. [very untidy; used of people's hair and appearance]

He **bears a striking resemblance to** his father. [looks remarkably like]

The lady who entered the room **had** a very **striking appearance**. [unusual appearance, in a positive, attractive sense]

TIP

Sometimes words are very restricted in what they can collocate with. The colour adjectives *blonde*, *ginger* and *auburn*[1] are only used of people's hair (not, for example, their clothes or other objects). When a word has restricted collocations, make a special note in your vocabulary notebook.
[1]reddish brown

Exercises

18.1 **Put the words from the box into the 'fat' or 'thin' column, then answer the questions.**

portly lanky slender dumpy slim chubby

'fat' words	*'thin' words*

1 Which words could be used to describe someone's waist?
2 Which word is likely to be used of a rather physically awkward young person?
3 Which word means 'fat but in a pleasant way'?
4 Which word is more likely to be used to describe a man rather than a woman?
5 Which word is more likely to be used to describe a woman rather than a man?

18.2 **Look at B. Then match the adjectives in the first box below with the nouns in the second box.**

bushy tiny oval striking broad droopy chubby dishevelled

cheeks moustache shoulders hair eyebrows resemblance tot face

18.3 **Fill the gaps with appropriate collocations. You are sometimes given the first letter(s).**

I hadn't seen Will since he was just a (1) t.................... t.................... , so I was surprised to see that he was now a tall young man. He was (2) im.................... gr.................... , smart and elegant. He was with a pretty young woman with (3) j....................-black, (4) shoulder-.................... hair and a (5) l.................... com.................... . She could have been a model, she had such a (6) str.................... ap.................... . He had his arm round her (7) s.................... wa.................... . With them was a (8) po.................... g.................... , who looked as though he enjoyed good food, and who was probably her father. When I introduced myself to Will, he smiled. 'Of course, I remember you,' he said. 'You used to work with my father. But you haven't aged at all! You have a much more (9) y.................... a.................... than my father now does. Dad has (10) .... very grey.' I felt very pleased when he said that; he obviously didn't notice I was beginning to (11) .... bald. Everyone likes to think they look young when they get older.

18.4 **Use the words from the box to fill the gaps to give contrasting meanings.**

round coarse upturned fair pointed straight dark sleek

1 Her hair's not ...., it's quite ...., in fact it's almost black.
2 She has an .... nose but her brother has a .... nose.
3 Her mother has a .... face but her father has a .... face.
4 My hair is so .... and ugly; Sally's is so .... and lovely.

FOLLOW UP Find a description of the hero or heroine in an English novel or short story. Note down any interesting collocations that you find there.

19 Families

A Family relationships

Sociologists talk about **nuclear** and **extended families**. A **nuclear family** is just parents and children. An **extended family** is a wider network including grandparents, cousins, etc.

Close relatives are those like parents, children, brothers or sisters. **Distant relatives** are people like **second cousins** [the children of a cousin of your mother or father] or **distant cousins.**

Close/immediate family refers to people who are your nearest **blood relatives:**
I don't have much **close/immediate family.**
She's a **distant cousin** of mine; she's not a **blood relative.**
Close can also be used to mean that the relationship is a very strong one:
We are a very **close family.** *or* We are a very **close-knit family.**

These adjectives also collocate with **family:**
loving, respectable, dysfunctional [unhappy, not working in a healthy way]
Simon came from a **respectable family,** so Mary's parents felt happy about the marriage.

Someone's **late husband/wife** is one who has died.
An **estranged** [formal] **husband/wife** is one who lives in a different place and has a difficult relationship with their husband/wife. They may be having a **trial separation** and may eventually decide to **get a divorce.** In some cases it can be a **bitter/acrimonious divorce.** [full of anger, arguments and bad feeling]
A person's **ex-husband/ex-wife** is a man/woman that she/he used to be married to.

Children whose parents have separated or divorced are said to come from a **broken home.** If their family is a strong, loving one it can be called a **stable home.** If it is a poor one, not having the things that are necessary for a pleasant life, such as enough money, food or good living conditions, it can be called a **deprived home.**

A **confirmed bachelor** is a man who seems to have no intention of ever marrying.

B Parents and children

collocation	*example*	*comment*
start a family	They are hoping to **start a family** soon.	NOT ~~begin~~ a family
have children	I'd like to **have** three **children**.	NOT ~~get~~ children
expect a baby	Soraya **is expecting a baby**.	NOT ~~wait (for)~~ a baby
have a baby	Jill **had her baby** yesterday.	NOT ~~get~~ a baby
the baby is due	The **baby is due** next week.	= expected to arrive
single parent/mother	It's hard being a **single parent**.	may be either unmarried or divorced
raise / bring up children / a family	Helen had to **bring up** four young **children** on her own.	*Raise a family* is more common in US than in UK English.
apply for custody of give/grant [formal] custody	The father **applied for custody of** the children, but the judge **gave/granted custody** to the mother.	*custody*: the legal right or duty to care for a child after its parents have separated or died
provide for your family	Nick works very long hours to **provide for his family**.	= to earn enough money to support your family
set up home	We live with my mum now, but we'll **set up home** on our own soon.	= to start an independent life in one's own flat or house

Exercises

19.1 **Fill the gaps in this old man's memories about his life with words from A.**

I grew up in an (1) .... family as my grandparents and a couple of aunts and an uncle, who was a (2) .... bachelor, lived with us. We saw a lot of our (3) .... relatives as well as our close ones. I think that families tended to be much more (4) .... then – we talked to each other more and did things together more. I'm sure there are far more (5) .... families now than there used to be – you know, where parents hardly spend any time with their children, or with each other – and a lot of parents who are divorced. My (6) .... wife, who died two years ago, used to say that it is not fair on children to let them grow up in (7) .... homes.

19.2 **Look at B. Correct the six collocation errors in this young woman's plans for the future.**

Charles and I are hoping to begin a family soon. We both want to get lots of children. Ideally, I'd like to have my first baby next year, when I'll be 25. My sister is waiting a baby now. It's coming next month. She's going to be a sole parent and it'll be hard for her to grow up a child on her own.

19.3 **Match the two parts of these collocations.**

1 apply for	cousin
2 get	separation
3 estranged	custody
4 nuclear	home
5 provide for	wife
6 distant	family
7 set up	your family
8 trial	a divorce

19.4 **Answer these questions.**

1 Who do you have in your immediate family?
2 Do you have much contact with your distant relatives? If so, when?
3 Where did your parents first set up home?
4 Which would most children prefer to live in, and why, a stable home or a deprived home?
5 What collocation means the same as *to be pregnant*?
6 Can dysfunctional families also be respectable ones?
7 What can be put before the words *wife* and *husband* to indicate that they are no longer married to someone?
8 What is a more formal alternative for *give custody*?

19.5 **Write a paragraph about your own family using as many as possible of the collocations from this unit.**

FOLLOW UP Read some English language women's magazines and note down any other interesting family collocations that you find.

20 Relationships

A Friendship

Here are some common collocations relating to friends and friendship.

collocation	*example*	*comment*
make friends	When you go to university you will **make** a lot of new **friends**.	NOT ~~find~~ friends (a common student error)
strike up a friendship	Jack **struck up a friendship** with a girl he met on holiday.	= start a friendship
form/develop a friendship	Juliet **formed a** lasting **friendship** with the boy she sat next to at primary school.	NOT ~~make~~ a friendship
cement/spoil a friendship	Spending several weeks on holiday together has **cemented their friendship**.	*cement* = strengthen spoil = have a bad effect on
a friendship grows	We were at school together, but our **friendship grew** after we'd left school.	*grow* = get stronger
close/special friends mutual friends	I'm glad that our children are such **close friends**, aren't you?	*mutual friends* = friends that you share with someone else
a casual acquaintance	I don't know Rod well. We're just **casual acquaintances**.	= someone you know a little
have a good relationship with someone	Anna and Marie **have a** very **good relationship**. They love doing things together.	NOT have a ~~relation / relations~~ with
keep in contact/ touch	We must **keep in contact** when the course ends.	opposite = **lose contact/touch**

B More than just good friends

A love story

I **fell madly in love with** Anton from the moment I met him. It was certainly **love at first sight**. I knew at once that he was **the love of my life** but at first I was not sure if my **love was returned** or not. Within a few days, however, he had told me that he was **desperately in love** with me too. A couple of weeks later, we realised that we wanted to **make a commitment** to each other and, when Anton asked me to marry him, I immediately **accepted his proposal**. I'm sure we will always **love each other unconditionally**[1]. Neither of us would ever consider **having an affair**[2] with someone else.

[1] love that is total and does not change regardless of what you or the **object of your love** does
[2] have a sexual relationship with someone outside marriage

Exercises

20.1 **Look at A. Choose an appropriate word to complete each sentence.**

1 Kay is quite a shy person and finds it hard to .... friends.
2 Do Paul and Sophie .... a good relationship?
3 Sam is always .... up friendships with people he meets on trains and planes.
4 I hope their disagreement over the bill won't .... their friendship.
5 It's amazing, when you meet someone new, how often you find that you have some .... friends.
6 Apparently, people .... most of their closest friendships when they are young.
7 I wouldn't call Graham a close friend, more a casual ....
8 We didn't really like each other at first, but our friendship .... as we got to know each other better.

20.2 **Make nine collocations out of the words in the box. Use each of the words once only.**

a	**a**	**a**	**accept**	**affair**	**an**	**at**
commitment	**contact**	**contact**	**first**	**friends**		
friendship	**have**	**in**	**keep**	**lose**	**make**	
love	**love**	**proposal**	**return**	**sight**		
someone's	**special**	**strike**	**up**			

20.3 **Answer these questions about the collocations on the opposite page.**

1 Which verb suggests that friendship can be seen as a plant?
2 Which collocation suggests that love is close to being crazy?
3 Which collocation from the love story means *agree to marry someone*?
4 Which collocation means the same as *special friends*?
5 Which collocation means the same as *keep in contact with*?

20.4 **Complete these questions. Then answer them.**

1 Have you ever fallen in love at first ....?
2 Do you think it's true that men are more reluctant to .... a commitment than women?
3 How old were you when you .... in love for the first time?
4 Do you think it is possible to have one person who is the love of your ....?
5 Have you ever been in love with someone who has not .... your love?
6 Do you think that men or women are more likely to be tempted to .... an affair?

20.5 **Look up these words in your dictionary. Note down two more good collocations for each one.**

love friend friendship relationship

21 Feelings and emotions

A Feeling happy

Look at these messages in cards sent to Brian and Helen on their wedding day. Note the collocations in bold.

Brian and Helen,
Have a great day. I know you'll be **blissfully**[1] **happy** together.
Simon

[1] very/extremely

To Brian and Helen –
Best wishes to **the happy couple**[2],
Jack

Dear Helen and Brian,
We hope marriage brings you **lasting happiness**.
Jake and Maria

Brian and Helen,
With love and best wishes on this **happy occasion**,
Uncle Eric

[2] a standard way of referring to a newly married couple

B Feeling sad and upset

In these letters to the problem page of Good Life magazine, useful collocations are in bold.

Dear Good Life,
My grandmother died six months ago and I've felt **desperately sad** and **deeply depressed** ever since. Is this normal for a 26-year-old?
Karen Young

Dear Good Life,
I felt a **great sadness** when I had to say goodbye to my friends at the end of our three years in university. The farewell party was such a **sad occasion**. What can I do? My life feels empty without them.
Jo Hart

Dear Good Life,
I was **bitterly**[1] **disappointed** recently when a friend **let me down badly**. How can I **express** my **disappointment** to her without appearing silly or childish? I'm not very good at **showing** my **feelings**.
Yolanda Reed

Dear Good Life,
I failed an exam recently and it was a **huge disappointment** to me. Now I'm feeling **increasingly anxious** that I'll fail the next one. In fact I'm **worried sick**. What should I do?
David Wright

[1]deeply disappointed is also common

C Anger and emotion

There is **mounting** [growing] **anger** over the new tax, along with **widespread condemnation** of it [a lot of people in many different places have condemned it]. It has especially **aroused feelings** of resentment among professional people.

I **lost my temper** and was **seething with anger** when she called me an idiot. [I suddenly became very angry]

Divorce is a **highly emotional** experience for all those involved. It's hard not to give a purely **emotional response**. The **emotional involvement** of both parties is intense, and the **emotional impact** on children is huge. [these are rather formal collocations]

Jack was an **emotional wreck** [informal: in a bad emotional state] after his girlfriend finished with him.

TIP This page gives a number of synonyms for *very/really/terribly* and for *big*, words which learners sometimes use too much. Make a special note of them.

Exercises

21.1 **How many words meaning *very* or *extremely* can you remember from the opposite page? Use them instead of *very* or *extremely* in these sentences.**

1 I was very disappointed. (give two answers)
2 Jess is a very emotional individual.
3 She felt extremely sad.
4 Her childhood was extremely happy.
5 I was extremely worried.
6 She felt very depressed.

21.2 **Improve the style of these e-mails by replacing the underlined words with collocations from the opposite page.**

Delete Reply Reply All Forward Print

1 Dear James
I have to tell you that there is general condemnation and growing anger over the news that the company pension scheme is to be closed down. The issue has brought out strong feelings among the staff. I am personally becoming more and more anxious that the situation might get out of control, and ask you to act immediately.
With best wishes,
Joanne Withers
Staff representative

2 Dear Joanne,
I too am full of anger over this pension question. I tried to show my disappointment over it to the Board, but they simply dismissed the issue and that just made me extremely angry. I feel very let down. I shall continue to do what I can.
Yours sincerely,
James Horgan (Resource Manager)

3 Gareth,
You probably know I didn't get the job I applied for. It's a very big disappointment.
Christina

4 Dear Winston,
I felt a big sadness when I heard of Patrick's death.
Will you be going to the funeral?
It will be such a sad thing, won't it?
Pamela

21.3 **Answer the questions.**

1 Give two examples of a happy occasion.
2 What phrase can refer to two people who have just got married?
3 What adjective collocates with *happiness* to mean 'which continues for many years'?
4 What other noun meaning 'effect' can collocate with *emotional*?
5 What is an informal way of saying *I was extremely worried*?

FOLLOW UP
Go to the Cambridge University Press website at www.cambridge.org and enter the word *temper* in the *Search Cambridge Dictionaries* box. Then click on *Look it up*. If you cannot use the web, look up *temper* in a good dictionary. What collocations can you find in addition to *lose your temper*?

22 Houses, flats and rooms

A Finding somewhere to live

Look at these notices on a university notice-board. Useful collocations are in bold.

Short-let[1] **accommodation** available near university. Rooms and **studio flats**[2]. Tel: 899544.

Are you looking to **move into a flat** or **house** next term? The Harmer Agency has a wide range of **suitable accommodation**. Call us on 4446677.

Fully furnished flat available to rent from 1st September. Quiet **residential area**. £800 per calendar month. Tel: 897633 after 5pm.

Newly-built apartment available soon. Spacious accommodation, **fully-fitted kitchen**[3]. **Off-road parking**. To let furnished or unfurnished. Would suit single academic or mature student. Tel: 3215786.

[1] can be rented for short periods of time
[2] small flats designed for one person
[3] kitchen that is already equipped with modern cooker, washing machine, cupboards, etc.

B Describing your house/flat/room

In these e-mails people are describing their living accommodation.

Delete Reply Reply All Forward Print

Hi Mave,
Luke and I have just moved into our **dream home**. It's a big old **four-storey house**. It's got a **spacious living room** which **has a** wonderful **view of** the park, and a **cosy study** where we can both work. And there are some lovely **light, airy bedrooms** which **overlook the garden**.
There is a separate **basement flat**, which we might **turn into a granny flat** for my mother. And if we want to **add an extension**[1] there's room for that too. It needs to be **completely refurbished**, but Luke and I have always wanted to **do up**[2] **an old house**.
Come and visit.
Love, Julia

Delete Reply Reply All Forward Print

Hi Julia,
You're so lucky! I'd love to **move out of** my awful one-room flat. It's in such a **dilapidated building**. You go into a **draughty hall**, down a **chilly corridor** and into this really **cramped room**. I want to buy **a place of my own** but there's a shortage of **affordable housing** here and I don't want to **take out** a big **mortgage**. I'd love to see your house. I hope you'll **invite me to** your **house-warming party**.
Big hug,
Mave

[1] we can also say **build an extension** = build an extra room or two onto an existing house
[2] repair, repaint and decorate (a house)

C Collocations with *home*

She **left home** to go to university, but moving away from her family made her **feel homesick**.

Peter's back from a year abroad. His family are throwing a party to **welcome him home**.

(To a guest who's just arrived) Come in and **make yourself at home** while I finish getting dinner ready. [relax and make yourself comfortable]

I haven't lived in Oxford for long but I already **feel at home** there.

I'd like to buy a **second home** near the coast. [house used only for weekends, holidays, etc.]

Exercises

22.1 Answer these questions using collocations from A.

1 What kind of accommodation would suit a student who has no furniture of his own?
2 What kind of accommodation would suit someone who is only going to be in a place for three months?
3 What part of town would you want to live in if you wanted to be somewhere where there are lots of private houses and no factories or other work places?
4 What kind of accommodation would suit a young single person who would prefer to live alone rather than to share?
5 If accommodation doesn't have its own garage, what else might it have to make life easier for car-owning residents?
6 If you are moving into a new unfurnished house, but don't need to take a washing machine, cooker or fridge with you, what does the house have?

22.2 Look at B. Match the beginning of each sentence on the left with its ending on the right.

1 We want to turn our garage into a	house-warming party.
2 Jill has invited me to her	mortgage.
3 Next week I have to move out of	my own.
4 Karl makes a business out of doing up	granny flat.
5 Our bedroom overlooks	my flat.
6 Our house needs to be completely	the garden.
7 I hope that one day I'll have a place of	old houses.
8 The bank can help if you want to take out a	refurbished.

22.3 Correct the collocation errors in these sentences.

1 We live on a busy road, but we're lucky because we have off-road park.
2 Gemma has moved off from her old flat and has now got a new place in Walville Street.
3 We're building an expansion to our house which will give us a bigger kitchen.
4 The flat is totally furnished, which is good because I have no furniture of my own.
5 She had to get out a big mortgage as the house was very expensive.
6 There is no buyable housing for young people in this area; prices are ridiculously high.
7 New people have entered into the house next door. I haven't met them yet.
8 It's a very spatial apartment with a huge living room and a big kitchen.
9 The flat is accessible to rent from the first of March onwards.
10 My brother and his wife live in a windy old cottage.

22.4 Replace the underlined words with collocations from the opposite page.

<u>The</u> home <u>you've always imagined</u> could be waiting for you at Highdale Cottages.
All cottages <u>let you see</u> the River Marn. Ideal for anyone seeking a <u>house used only for weekends or holidays</u> in the area.
Telephone 3340251 for appointments to view.

22.5 Complete these sentences using collocations from C opposite.

1 Jane's been away a whole year and now she's back. We should have a party to ....
2 Our son lives at home right now but he'll be 21 soon. He'll finish university and then he'll probably ....
3 I've lived here almost a year now and I'm really beginning to ....
4 I'll leave the keys to my flat with the neighbour. Just go in and ....
5 Jane thought she would miss her friends and family when she started her new job in Rome but she soon found she had no time to ....

23 Eating and drinking

A Talking about types of food

In each of these conversations, useful collocations are in bold.

Tom: Kids eat far too much **junk food**.
Nelly: Yeah, but it's hard to get them to eat **nourishing meals**[1]. They think they're boring.

[1] meals which make you healthy and strong

Fran: Have you tried the new supermarket yet?
Jim: Yes. The **fresh produce**[2] is excellent, and they have a big **organic food** section.
Fran: Mm, yes. I actually think their **ready meals**[3] are good too.

[2] foods produced from farming, e.g. dairy produce, agricultural produce; pronounced /ˈprɒdjuːs/
[3] meals already prepared or which just need to be heated quickly before eating

Liam: I can't believe **food additives**[4] are good for our long-term health.
Todd: No, and I think **processed foods**[5] in general are probably bad for us, not to mention **GM foods**[6]!

[4] substances added to food to improve its taste or appearance or to preserve it
[5] foods which are changed or treated as part of an industrial operation
[6] genetically modified foods

Gail: The restaurant was leaving **perishable food**[7] lying round outside the fridge, and some people got **food poisoning** so the authorities closed it down.
Terry: Oh dear.

[7] food which goes bad quickly, e.g. cheese, fish

B Eating and drinking

Look at this information on eating out for visitors to a town. Note the collocations in bold.

> Whether it's a **light meal** or a **substantial**[1] **meal** you're looking for, whether you want a **slap-up meal**[2], a **gourmet**[3] **meal** or just tasty, **home-cooked food**, there's something for everyone in the Old Port restaurant area. Enjoy good food in a pleasant setting.

[1] large [2] unusually large and good [3] high-quality

Jane and Ron are in the Old Port restaurant area looking for somewhere to eat.

Jane: Let's find a café and **have a quick snack**. And I could really do with a **refreshing drink**.
Ron: I'm **dying of hunger**! I need a **square meal**.
Jane: I know you have a **healthy appetite**, but you had a **hearty breakfast** only three hours ago! Well, how about having a **soft drink** and a bag of crisps now, and a proper lunch later?
Ron: Crisps will only **spoil your appetite**. Look, this restaurant looks good and the **set menu** is **reasonably priced**. Let's go in.

> **ERROR WARNING**
> We say **international food/cuisine**, NOT ~~world-wide~~ food/cuisine. A Chinese/Mexican/French **meal** is what you eat in a restaurant. When referring in general to the food of a country or culture we say Chinese/Mexican/French **food/cooking/cuisine**.

Exercises

23.1 Match the words on the left with their collocations on the right.

1 set	additives
2 food	food
3 junk	produce
4 ready	menu
5 fresh	meals

23.2 Complete these sentences using the collocations from exercise 23.1 to fill the gaps.

1 .... such as artificial flavours and colouring can cause allergies.
2 .... may be unhealthy, but it's quick and easy and fills you up.
3 People who don't have much time to cook often buy .... from the supermarket.
4 It's always better to buy .... instead of canned or frozen foods.
5 The .... is usually cheaper than ordering dishes separately in a restaurant.

23.3 Read these remarks by different people, then answer the questions.

Richard: I've got some cheese and milk. Is there a fridge here I could put them in?
Archie: I feel so hungry! I can't believe it!
Polly: I've been sick and my stomach is aching. Must be something I ate.
Ken: No matter how much I eat, I always want more.
Suzie: All these vegetables have been grown without any chemicals at all.
Nina: I always enjoy my food and look forward to it.

	name
1 Who has organic food?	
2 Who has an insatiable appetite?	
3 Who has perishable food?	
4 Who has a healthy appetite?	
5 Who has food poisoning?	
6 Who is dying of hunger?	

23.4 Replace the underlined words with suitable collocations from the opposite page.

1 Foods which are changed or treated as part of an industrial operation may damage our health in the long term.
2 Some people always have three full, satisfying meals a day, but I prefer a large breakfast and then a small meal around midday and a more sizeable meal in the evening.
3 There are some overpriced restaurants in the city centre, but down at the beach, there are some nice, not too expensively priced ones.
4 On my birthday my parents took me out for a big, good meal. They wanted to go for a very high quality meal but I said I'd prefer something more ordinary.
5 Iced tea is a drink that cools you and makes you feel less tired on a hot day, and is probably better for you than non-alcoholic drinks such as cola or lemonade.
6 Let me take you out to dinner on your birthday. Or would you prefer a meal prepared at home? I could make dinner for you at my place.

24 Films and books

A Talking about films and books

When a new **book** or **film comes out**, newspapers will review it. The people who **review the book/film** are called **book reviewers / film critics** and they write **book/film reviews.** If they don't like a book/film they **give it a bad review.** We can say that a novel or film is **based on a true story.** We say that a **book/film captures** an atmosphere or that a **book/film deals with** a topic. We talk about the **opening/closing scenes** of a film and the **opening/closing chapters** of a book. We talk about the **beginning** and **end of a book/film** (NOT ~~start~~ and ~~finish~~). If everything works out well for the **central characters**, we say that the book/film **has a happy ending.** You may **recommend a book/film** that you enjoyed to a friend. If a lot of people have enjoyed it, it is **highly recommended.**

B Just about films and acting

I've never had any desire to **go on the stage**[1] myself but I'd love to produce a film. I think historical dramas work particularly well on **the big screen**[2] and I'd love to make a film about Vikings in Britain. There'd be plenty of opportunities to use **special effects**[3] during battle scenes. I'd want the **male lead**[4] to be played by Hugh Grant, while Nicole Kidman could have the **female lead.** Sean Penn could **play the role of** a Viking warrior and I'd like Judi Dench to take on a **cameo role**[5]. I'm sure that, as always, she would **give** an excellent **performance.** My dream is to make a film that would be **nominated for an Oscar**[6]. Of course, I'd also like it to be an immediate **box-office hit**[7], playing to **full houses**[8] worldwide.

1 become an actor
2 the cinema
3 powerful visual effects, often created using technology
4 main male part
5 small but special part
6 put on the official list of people in the film world who may receive a special prize (an Oscar)
7 extremely successful with audiences
8 cinemas/theatres with no empty seats

Other strong collocations are **cast a film** [select the actors for a film], **star in a film, shoot a film, make a film.**

C Just about books

collocation	*example*
be engrossed/absorbed in a book	Sal was so **engrossed/absorbed in her book** that she didn't hear me.
compulsive reading	Many people find articles about the private lives of film stars **compulsive reading**. [so interesting you can't stop reading]
bedtime reading	I don't think a horror story makes good **bedtime reading**.
an easy read	Detective stories are good for train journeys as they're **an easy read**.
take out / borrow / return / renew a library book	You can **take out/borrow** six **library books** at one time. You should **return your library book** tomorrow. I'm going to **renew my library book** for another week.
flick/skim through a book	Mona **flicked/skimmed through the book** without reading it in detail.
beautifully written	The book is **beautifully written** – I highly recommend it.

ERROR WARNING

Critics **review** books and films, NOT ~~criticise~~ them. To *criticise* a book or film means to say negative things about it.
Remember that you **watch television**, NOT ~~see~~ television, but you can **see** or **watch a film** or **programme** on television. We usually say **see a film** at the cinema.

Exercises

24.1 **Use collocations from A opposite instead of the underlined words in this conversation. The conversation has no errors, but the changes will improve it.**

Matthew: Have you read that new book that has just appeared about Ireland?
Lorna: No, I don't go to bookshops and I don't read articles discussing new books. What's it about?
Matthew: Well, it concerns the Irish War of Independence. It's very authentic and it manages to give the atmosphere of Ireland at the beginning of the 20th century.
Lorna: Is it just historical facts, then?
Matthew: No, the main people are two brothers who have different opinions about the war and this divides their family. In the first chapters they're happy and do everything together, but by the last chapter they have become enemies.
Lorna: Mm, it sounds a bit depressing to me.
Matthew: Well, it certainly doesn't finish in a happy way, but I liked it, and it's recommended very much by all the critics.
Lorna: So, a book with a pleasant start and a sad finish. Not for me, I'm afraid. I prefer the opposite.

24.2 **Complete the crossword.**

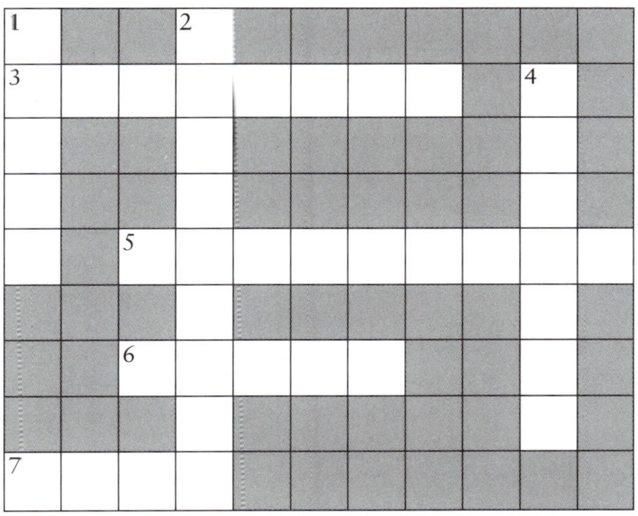

Across
3 I was completely .... in my book and didn't realise how late it had got.
5 An alternative to 3 across.
6 He wants to go on the .... He's always wanted to be an actor.
7 Who played the male .... in *Destination Saturn*?

Down
1 .... role means 'small but special part in a film/play'.
2 The film was .... for an Oscar but it didn't win.
4 It was an amazing film about space travel, with fantastic special ....

24.3 **Match the words in the box on the left with their collocations on the right.**

full big bedtime female box-office

screen reading lead hit house

24.4 **Complete these collocations.**

1 shoot / star in / make a ....
2 renew / borrow / return a ....
3 flick / skim through a ....
4 compulsive / bedtime ....

FOLLOW UP Online bookshops, for example, *Amazon*, often have mini-reviews and descriptions of books and DVDs. Find a review of a book or film that you know and note down any interesting collocations in it.

25 Music

A Describing music

Look at these music reviews and note the collocations in bold.

Bloom ***Music from the Centre of the Earth***
(Palm records 234655)

New arrivals on the rock **music scene**, Bloom are already making a big impact. If you're looking for **background music**, then this is not for you, but if you want **music** to **blast out from**[1] your hi-fi and annoy the neighbours, then Bloom's **debut**[2] **album**, with tracks from their **live performance** at the Delaya Stadium, may be just what you want.

Johnny MacRoy ***Songs we loved***
(Kase Phonograph 488792)

For fans of **easy listening**[3] and **catchy**[4] **tunes**, this is all you need. In fact it's so relaxing you might just fall asleep. MacRoy **gives a** sentimental **performance** of these old love songs. At 47, he's not exactly a **pop idol** but his **adoring fans** will love it.

The Divide ***Amphibian***
(Fono Corp 3321978)

This is a rock symphony, an extraordinary **piece of music**. After their **massive hit** in 2004 with *Megalith*, their record company has **released** this **CD** hoping for another **big hit**. The band themselves **wrote the music**. They have a **huge following** and are due to **go on tour** later this year.

The Oxbridge Symphonia ***British classics old and new*** **(Rotor Records 775537)**

Haunting melodies and the occasional **virtuoso**[5] **performance** from its two soloists mark this collection of popular British classical music, which aims to **capture a wider audience** for the classics and to promote Britain's **musical heritage**. Roger Crow **conducts the orchestra**. Crow himself **composed** two of the **pieces**, hence the CD title. Good birthday present for your uncle and aunt. But if you're a real classical **music lover**, save your money.

BUST-OUT WITH JOLA V ***BLAZE MAMA***
(Presto 58843)

Bust-out's new double **CD features**[6] **Jola V**, a young **rap**[7] **artist** from Miami. Jola used to be with Chicago hip-hop band Frenzy, but **went solo** in 2004. The band have **remixed**[8] four tracks from earlier albums and Jola's **up-tempo**[9] numbers just add to the excitement.

1 sound extremely loud
2 presented to the public for the first time
3 music that is not serious or difficult
4 pleasant and easy to remember
5 extremely skilful
6 includes as an important part
7 rock music in which rhymed lyrics are spoken over rhythm tracks
8 made a new version of a musical track
9 played at a fast beat

B Playing music

Exercises

25.1 **Change the underlined words using collocations from A so that each sentence has the opposite meaning.**

1 The band's last CD was a <u>minor</u> hit. (give two answers)
2 There are some great <u>slow</u> numbers on this new CD.
3 The band has a <u>small</u> following of dedicated fans.
4 Music was <u>playing quietly on</u> a CD player when I entered the house.
5 Maria Plurosa gave a <u>poor</u> performance of Heder's violin concerto last night.

25.2 **Correct the eight collocation errors in this paragraph. The first one is done for you.**

For all folk music ~~likers,~~ Johnny Coppin's new CD, *The Long Harvest*, published last week, will be a great addition to their collection. Bob recently got solo after five years with the folk band Blue Mountain. He is proud of the musical inheritance of his native Kentucky. Tracks 3 and 7 comprise his old friend Wiz Carter on guitar. With this CD Coppin says he hopes to control a wider audience for folk music. His excellent living performance at the recent Lockwood Folk Festival suggests he has a good chance of succeeding. He makes a tour next month. Don't miss him.

1	lovers
2	
3	
4	
5	
6	
7	
8	

25.3 **What word(s) mean ...?**

1 ... music that is playing while you are doing something else and not really listening to it?
2 ... music that is not complicated or difficult to listen to?
3 ... a pop musician who is a very big star with many fans?
4 ... a type of performer who speaks rhymed lyrics over rhythm tracks?
5 ... to tighten or loosen the strings of an instrument till they make the correct note?
6 ... a way of playing a guitar by moving your fingers across the strings?

25.4 **Complete these sentences with suitable collocations.**

1 Hundreds of .... fans were waiting for Shamira to come out of the concert hall.
2 The orchestra gave a wonderful .... of some popular classics.
3 It was a very .... tune; you only had to hear it once and you were singing it.
4 I'd love to .... a musical instrument but I don't have time.
5 It is one of those .... melodies which you never forget, so beautiful, yet so sad.
6 There's a lot of musical .... in the family; all the children play an instrument.

26 Sport

A Do, *play* and *go*

The table below gives examples of common sporting collocations with *do*, *play* and *go*.

You **do**	gymnastics, judo, weightlifting, aerobics, yoga, wrestling, circuit training, archery, athletics
You **play**	games, badminton, billiards, hockey, bowls, rugby, golf, (table) tennis, cricket, baseball, chess, darts, cards, dominoes
You **go**	fishing, skiing, bowling, cycling, skateboarding, surfing, snowboarding, hang-gliding, climbing, hill walking, sailing, jogging, swimming

You can also say you **go to aerobics/judo/yoga/karate** – this means that you go to a class in this sport.

ERROR WARNING

Learners often make mistakes with some common collocations connected with sport. Make a point of learning these commonly used collocations.

- You **do** or **play sport**. (NOT ~~make~~ sport)
- You **do exercises**. (NOT ~~make~~ exercises)
- You **play computer** or other **games**. (NOT ~~do~~ games)
- You **have/play a game of** cards. (NOT ~~make~~ a game)
- You **go skiing**. (NOT ~~make~~ skiing)
- You **do activities**. (NOT ~~make~~ or ~~practise~~ activities)

If you are a serious sportsperson, you will certainly practise your sport, but that has a specific meaning, which is to do something again and again in order to get better at it, in other words **to train**. If you are a footballer you might **practise taking a penalty**, for example.

B Winning and losing

Sportsmen and sportswomen want to **win matches**, not **lose matches**. But you can't win all the time! Sometimes a team or player **deserves to win**, but gets **narrowly defeated/beaten**.

Before they **go in for / enter a competition**, athletes **train hard**. They probably **attend/do** at least five **training sessions** a week. They are likely to **put up a fight** to **gain/get a place** in the next **stage/round of the competition**. Of course, a sportsperson's ultimate aim is to **break the world record** in their sport. If they succeed, they **set a new world record** and become a **world record holder**. They are sure to **come up against fierce/intense competition** as they try to **achieve their ambitions**. Sometimes they are satisfied if they just **achieve a personal best**.

Some sports people so **desperately want** to win that they take drugs to **enhance their performance**. This will be discovered when they **fail a drugs test**.

C Football

You can **play** or **have a (football) match / game (of football)**. It might be a **home** or an **away match** depending on whether you're playing on your team's **home ground** or not.

The aim is to **score a goal**. Players may **tackle an opponent** to try to **take possession of the ball**[1]. If you tackle in an illegal way, you **foul your opponent**. This will lead to the referee **blowing his whistle** and an opponent **taking a penalty** or **taking a free kick**. If someone isn't playing very well the manager may decide to **drop the player** from the team or **bring on a substitute**[2]. Both teams hope that they will have **taken the lead**[3] by half-time.

[1] get the ball [2] replace one player with another [3] be in a winning position

Exercises

26.1 Look at A. Complete the sentences with *do*, *play* or *go* in the correct form.

New Sports Club Opening Next Week

You can .... judo! You can .... badminton!

You can .... swimming! You can .... weight lifting!

You can .... circuit training! You can .... table tennis!

You can .... skateboarding! You can even .... darts!

In fact, you can .... almost any sport you can think of. So join now!

26.2 Look at B and C. Make ten collocations by matching a word from the box on the left with a word or phrase from the box on the right.

personal	set
blow	achieve
bring on	train
fail	enhance
enter	take

the lead	a competition
best	your performance
a substitute	a drugs test
a record	hard
a whistle	your ambitions

26.3 Look at the error warning. There are six verb + noun errors in this e-mail. Find and correct them.

Delete Reply Reply All Forward Print

Hi, Jose,

Do you fancy coming on a sporting weekend with me next month? It sounds great – would make a change from playing computer games. You can make lots of different activities. You could even do fishing, I think. You can't go skiing at this time of year but you can make water skiing, if you like. Everyone has to make general exercises first thing in the morning and then you can make whatever sport you like, more or less. I've never practised badminton so I think I'm going to do that. Then in the afternoon I'm looking forward to the chance to practise my tennis serve with their professional coach. Please try to come!

Giorgio

26.4 Complete the collocations in this report of a rugby match.

Cambridge were happy to (1) .... their last match 6:0. Oxford, the opposing team, put up a good (2) .... and some people thought they (3) .... to win. They were fearless in (4) .... their opponents, but every time they took (5) .... of the ball, Cambridge managed to win it back. Cambridge have now (6) .... a place in the next (7) .... of the competition. They will undoubtedly come up against some fierce (8) .... However, they have already managed to (9) .... an interesting world record by having four members of the same family in their winning team!

FOLLOW UP Make a section in your vocabulary notebook for your own favourite sport. Find an English language website connected with that sport. Write down any useful collocations you notice there.

27 Health and illness

A Verb collocations referring to illnesses and injuries

In most everyday situations you can use the verbs *get* or *have* with the names of illnesses, but you will improve your written style if you can use these alternative verbs and expressions.

verb	*common collocations*	*example*
catch	a cold, the flu, a chill, pneumonia	I got soaking wet and **caught a cold**.
contract [formal]	a disease, malaria, typhoid	Uncle Jess **contracted malaria** while he was working in Africa.
develop [formal]	(lung/breast) cancer, diabetes, AIDS, arthritis, Alzheimer's disease	My grandfather **developed Alzheimer's disease** and could no longer remember things or recognise people.
suffer from	asthma, hay fever, backache	She has **suffered from asthma** all her life.
have an attack of	bronchitis, asthma, hay fever, diarrhoea	She **had an attack of hay fever** and was sneezing non-stop.
be diagnosed with	(lung/breast) cancer, AIDS, leukaemia, autism	He was **diagnosed with lung cancer** and died a year later.
suffer / sustain [formal]	(major/minor/serious/head) injuries	The driver **sustained serious head injuries** in the crash.

B Fitness and good health

Look at this magazine questionnaire and note the collocations relating to fitness.

Are you in **good shape**?

1 Do you **take** regular **vigorous exercise**? ☐
2 Do you eat a **balanced diet**? ☐
3 Do you care about **healthy eating**? ☐
4 Do you **follow** a personal **fitness programme**? ☐
5 Do you always **stick to your programme**? ☐
6 In general, have you **kept fit** over the last two years? ☐

C Talking about sickness and pain

My poor friend Gina is **terminally ill**. [She will die soon.] She suffers **excruciating/unbearable pain** most of the time. Apparently it's an **incurable illness** that runs in her family.
Paul annoys everyone at work. He takes days off even for the most **trivial/minor ailments**.
It's a **serious illness**, but probably not **life-threatening**.
For a few days it was **acutely/intensely painful**, but now it's just a **dull ache**. My doctor **prescribed** me **some tablets** and they **relieved/alleviated the pain**.
Lorna was **taken ill** the other day. She's in hospital. They're not sure what it is yet.
I had a **heavy cold** and a **splitting headache**, so I wasn't in a good mood. [the opposite of a heavy cold is a **slight cold**]

ERROR WARNING
In accidents, wars, etc., **things** get **damaged** and **people** get **injured**:
Their **car was slightly damaged** but luckily **no one was injured**.

Exercises

27.1 **Look at A. Match the verbs and expressions on the left with their collocations on the right.**

1 sustain	diarrhoea
2 contract	a cold
3 have an attack of	breast cancer
4 develop	minor injuries
5 be diagnosed with	typhoid
6 catch	autism

27.2 **Use the verbs and expressions in the left-hand column of exercise 27.1 instead of the verb *get* in these newspaper extracts.**

1 Many musicians who get arthritis experience the tragedy of no longer being able to play their instrument.

2 More than 50 passengers on the flight got moderate or severe diarrhoea. Medical officials suspect the in-flight catering was responsible.

3 To get cancer is the most frightening experience, and people often need intense counselling to cope with it.

4 Millions of people get malaria each year in poorer countries, and drugs to treat it are in short supply.

5 Mr Taylor escaped with bruises, but experts say he was lucky not to have got serious injuries.

6 Patients often get pneumonia while in hospital. In fact, experts now think hospitals may be the worst place to be if you are sick and weak.

27.3 **Complete the collocations. You are given the first letter of the missing words.**

1 Flu is not a s.................... illness for most people, but it can be l....................-t.................... for elderly people who are weak and who haven't been vaccinated.
2 Patients who are t.................... ill often prefer to die at home surrounded by their loved ones.
3 I'm not in pain, it's just a d.................... ache in my back tooth. I hate going to the dentist's.
4 The children have a b.................... diet, with lots of fruit and vegetables and only a few sweet things now and then.
5 Turn that music down! I've got a s.................... headache!
6 You shouldn't waste the doctor's time with t.................... ailments. Get something at the chemist's instead.
7 I need to adopt a proper fitness programme and to s.................... to it to get into shape again. I was in good s.................... a year ago but then I became a bit lazy.
8 Diseases which are i.................... now will be beaten one day if scientists continue to make progress with drugs and genetic science.
9 My aunt was t.................... ill when she was on holiday. Apparently, she was in e.................... pain. Luckily she had travel insurance.
10 I believe in h.................... eating and I try to do v.................... exercise every other day.
11 My doctor p.................... me a new drug to a.................... my backache. It worked!
12 I took a day off work yesterday. It was nothing serious, just a s.................... cold.

FOLLOW UP

If you have not already done it, complete the questionnaire at B opposite. If you think you need to change your habits, make a note of it, e.g. *Take more vigorous exercise!*

28 Computers

A E-mail and the Internet

Look at these conversations where people are asking for assistance at an Internet café.

Customer: How do I **go online**?
Assistant: You're already **connected to the Internet**. Do you want to **send e-mail**?
Customer: No, I just want to **browse the web** for a while.
Assistant: OK, just open the **search engine** or **enter the web address** and **press 'enter'**.

Customer: I can't **access** my company's **website**. Can you help?
Assistant: Have you **put in** the correct **address**?
Customer: Yes, I'm sure I have.

Customer: How do I **reply to this e-mail**? Sorry, I'm not very good with computers.
Assistant: That's OK. Just **hit 'reply'**, then **compose your message**, then **press 'send'**.
Customer: Then can I **forward the message** to myself at my **home address**?
Assistant: Yes. Make sure you enter the right address, or the **e-mail will bounce** [come back]. Let me know if you would like a **hard copy** of your e-mail and I'll show you how to **print out your work**. [a copy on paper]

Customer: What do I do if I want to **download this picture**?
Assistant: You have to **save it to a disk**. I can sell you one if you don't have one.

Customer: Can I **send an attachment** with this e-mail?
Assistant: Yes, you click here and then **attach the file**.

Customer: I'd like to **visit a chat room**. Is that OK?
Assistant: No problem. **Select this option** here. Then just ask if you need my help.

B Some advantages and disadvantages of computers today

+ On the web you can **access information** on any subject you want to.
– As well as getting useful e-mails, you also **receive** a lot of **spam**. [junk e-mails]
+ Good web design is making it easier to **navigate websites**. [find your way round]
– Computer criminals are getting better at **hacking into** other people's **computers**. [illegally going into other people's computer files]
+ People are **maintaining** their **web pages** better, so information is kept up-to-date.
– **Computers** still **crash** and you have to waste time **re-installing** your **programs**.
+ **Broadband connections** are widely available now. This makes **online shopping** much easier.
– Whenever you need to do something really important at work, the **computers** seem to **be down**. [not be working]
+ **Burning a CD** is a quick and easy way to **back up your work**.
– It is very easy to accidentally **delete** or **erase a file**. [get rid of / destroy a file]
+ Being able to **hold records on computer** makes it much easier for businesses to keep track of customers and of orders.

C Mobile phone technology

My new mobile's great. I love **using predictive text** now. The screen is small but it **displays images** brilliantly. I've got some fantastic **ring tones**. I can **record** short **video clips** and send them to my friends and I can **access** my **e-mails** on it. I've **downloaded** some new **games** with **great graphics** on it. I use it all the time but I hardly ever make calls on it!

Exercises

28.1 **Look at A. Match the words on the left with their collocations on the right.**

1 browse	a file
2 be connected	online
3 enter	to the Internet
4 access	a chat room
5 compose	the web
6 attach	a website
7 go	an option
8 visit	the web address
9 select	a message

28.2 **Choose the correct collocation.**

1 It is very important for websites to be *maintained / hacked into*.
2 Sam spends hours every evening *accessed / connected* to the Internet.
3 I don't *crash / receive* as much spam as I used to.
4 Is it an easy website to *navigate / reinstall*?
5 How can I *burn / enter* a CD on this computer?
6 It's a good idea to keep a *hard / fast* copy of all important documents.
7 Be very careful not to *select / delete* your work.
8 Do you do a lot of *computer / online* shopping?

28.3 **Answer this computer quiz using collocations from the opposite page.**

1 What may you have to do with your computer programs if your computer crashes?
2 What must you do regularly so you don't lose the document you are working on?
3 What must you be careful not to do accidentally?
4 What should you check if you're not able to access a web page you want to look at?
5 What is Google?
6 If you don't put the right address on an e-mail, what will happen?
7 How do you reply to an e-mail that you have received?
8 If you want to get a picture from the Internet and save it to your own computer, what do you have to do?
9 If you want to send a message you have received on to someone else, what do you do?
10 If you want to e-mail a document to someone, what do you normally do?
11 If you want to work on a document at home, where will you e-mail the document?
12 What feature on a mobile phone allows you to text someone more rapidly?

28.4 **Complete these sentences.**

1 Her phone has got a very irritating .... tone.
2 Has your computer got a broadband .... ?
3 Some people think that too many records about us are .... on computer these days.
4 Did you read about that teenager who .... into the Pentagon's main computer?
5 I want a mobile phone that will let me .... my e-mails when I am away from home.
6 My sister e-mailed me this wonderful video .... of her new baby.
7 This computer screen has great resolution and so displays .... very well.
8 In this computer exercise you have to .... the right answer, A, B, C or D.

FOLLOW UP

Go to the website of the make of computer or mobile phone that you use. Select a page that interests you – perhaps something about a new product. Make a note of any interesting collocations that you see there.

29 Study and learning

A Alternatives to *do* and *get*

You can improve your written style by using alternative collocations instead of *do* and *get*.

expression with **do/get**	*alternatives*
do an exam	I have to **sit/take an exam** in biology at the end of term.
do research, do a research project	Our class **carried out / conducted a research project** into the history of our school.
do a course	I decided to **enrol on / take** a course in computer programming.
do a degree/diploma	She **studied for / took** a degree in engineering.
do a subject (e.g. law)	I **studied/took history and economics** in high school.
do an essay/assignment	All students have to **write an essay/assignment** at the end of term.
do a lecture/talk	Professor Parkinson **gave a lecture** on the American Civil War.
get a degree/diploma	He **obtained / was awarded a diploma** in Town Planning in 1998.
get a grade	Her essay **received / was given** an A-grade.
get a qualification	You will need to **obtain/acquire a qualification** in social work.
get an education	The country is poor; only 27% of children **receive** a basic **education**.

ERROR WARNING

Don't confuse **pass an exam** with **sit/take an exam**. *Pass* means to be successful in an exam or test.
Say 'I **did** my homework', NOT 'I ~~made~~ my homework.'

B

Look at these conversations between a teacher and students. Note how the teacher uses more formal collocations to repeat what each student says.

Student: Do we have to **go to** all **the lectures** to **do the course** or just yours?
Teacher: You must **attend** all **the lectures** to **complete the course**.

Student: Excuse me. Where will next week's **class be**? In this room?
Teacher: No. Next week's **class will be held** in Room 405.

Student: When do we have to **give** you **our essays**?
Teacher: You have to **hand in your essays** on Friday.

Student: When do we have to **send in our** university **applications**?
Teacher: You have to **submit your application** by December 1st.

Student: What do I have to do if I want to **leave the course**?
Teacher: If you want to **withdraw from the course**, you have to go to the College Office.

C More collocations connected with study and learning

Do you **keep a** vocabulary **notebook**? It's a good way of recording new collocations.
I did the **first draft** of my essay last week and the **final draft** this week. I have to hand it in tomorrow. Then the teacher **gives** us **feedback** after about a week.
We don't have exams at my school. We have **continuous assessment**. [system where the quality of a student's work is judged by pieces of course work and not by one final examination]
The local technical college **provides training** for young people in a variety of professions.
After secondary school, 30% of the population go on to **higher/tertiary education**, and 20% of adults do some sort of **further education** course during their lives.
Does your government **recognise** foreign **qualifications** for school teachers?

Exercises

29.1 Replace all the uses of *do* or *get* in this paragraph with more interesting words.

I have three daughters. The oldest one did a degree in economics at Birmingham University. She got her bachelor's degree last year and is now doing some research on taxation laws in different countries. The second one is doing a course at Newcastle University. She's doing history. She loves it, though she says she has to do far too many assignments. My youngest daughter is still at school. She's doing her school-leaving exams in the summer. She'll go to university next year if she gets good enough grades in her exams. She wants to do sociology and then get a social work qualification. My daughters are all getting a much better education than I ever had.

29.2 Complete these questions.

1 What homework do we have to .... tonight?
2 In which month do students usually .... their final exams in your country?
3 Who do we have to .... our essays in to?
4 Who is .... today's lecture on Shakespeare?
5 What do we need to do if we want to .... from the course?
6 In which room is the translation class going to be ....?
7 Have you done the first .... of your essay yet?
8 Do you prefer exams or continuous ....?
9 Do you always .... to all your lectures?
10 Does the college .... training in computer skills?

29.3 Choose the correct collocation.

1 I'm happy to say that you have all *sat / taken / passed* your maths test.
2 Will the teacher *give / provide / make* us some feedback on our essays?
3 The university *agrees / recognises / takes* the school-leaving exams of most other countries.
4 It isn't compulsory to *assist / attend / listen* all the lectures at this university.
5 How long will it take you to *complete / carry out / fulfil* your degree?
6 You must *submit / send / write* your application in before the end of June.
7 Several students have decided to *withdraw / go / leave* the course this year.
8 I want you all to *write / hold / keep* a vocabulary notebook.

29.4 Answer these questions about education.

1 At what age do children in your country sit their final school exams?
2 How long does it take in your country to do a degree in medicine?
3 Give one advantage you think continuous assessment has over traditional exams.
4 What sort of feedback might a teacher give a student who has just given a presentation in class?
5 Give one advantage for a learner of English of doing homework.
6 What advice about keeping a vocabulary notebook would you give to someone starting to learn English?
7 What is the difference between further education and higher or tertiary education?
8 What would you expect to be the difference between the first draft of an essay and the final draft?

30 Work

A Jobs, career and work

JOB
- a fulfilling job
- a high-powered job[1]
- a demanding job
- to apply for a job
- a steady job
- to offer someone a job
- a permanent job

WORK
- to carry out work
- to supervise work
- to complete work
- to work closely with
- available to start work
- to take on work

CAREER
- to wreck/ruin someone's career
- to embark on a career[2]
- at the height/peak of your career
- to have a career in (medicine)
- her career lasted ...
- a brilliant career
- to climb the career ladder
- a promising career
- a career takes off[3]

Note we say **have a job**, NOT have a ~~work~~.

[1] an important job
[2] to start a career
[3] a career starts to become very successful

B Job adverts

Do you **have a good knowledge of** the fashion industry?
Do you **have experience in** sales?
Are you a **good team player**[1]?
Are you looking for a **stimulating working environment**?
Would you like to be an **integral part** of a **close team**?
We can offer you **job satisfaction** and **generous benefits**[2].
Vacancy must be filled[3] within three weeks.
For further details, phone 08965 439820.

[1] a person who co-operates well with other people
[2] good rewards for work – not just salary but also perhaps a company car, good holiday entitlement, etc.
[3] the job must be offered to someone and accepted

C Things you might do at work

Bella **has a job as** a PA. Basically her role is to **take charge of** her boss, who is not a very organised person, and make sure nothing **goes wrong**. She **makes appointments** for her boss and she makes sure he **keeps his appointments**. She spends a lot of time **answering the phone** and **fielding telephone calls**[1] on his behalf. When her boss has to travel, she **makes the reservations** for him. When her boss has to **give a presentation**, she **makes** all **the preparations** that are required, including **making photocopies** of any papers that he needs. She **arranges meetings** for him and she **takes the minutes**[2] at the meetings. Bella is a very well-organised person. She **keeps a record** of everything she does at work and **sets** herself **targets**. She does her best to **achieve her goals**. Every morning she **makes a list** of everything she needs to do. Today the first thing on her list is **'Hand in my notice'**[3]! But she's not going to **take early retirement**. She's got a new job where she will be the boss and will have her own PA.

[1] dealing with all the calls she can handle herself and only putting the most urgent ones through to her boss
[2] keeps the official record of a meeting
[3] resign, inform her boss she's planning to stop working for him

Exercises

30.1 **Complete the sentences with *work*, *job* or *career*.**

1 I took on too much .... last month and couldn't finish it all.
2 At the peak of her .... she was managing a sales force of 200 people.
3 Daniel Robertson's .... in education lasted almost four decades.
4 I have a very demanding ...., but I enjoy it, nonetheless.
5 At the moment we are carrying out .... on the design of the new stadium.
6 The scandal ruined his .... and he never worked in the stock market again.
7 I'm going to apply for a .... in a supermarket.
8 She had a long and brilliant .... in show business. At 20, she got her first steady .... in a small regional theatre, but it was in 1968 that her .... really took off when she was offered a part in a TV series.

30.2 **Look at this job advert, then look at the shortlist of candidates below. Rank them in order of suitability for the job, from 1 (most suitable) to 3 (least suitable), and give your reasons.**

The Carlsson Group: Marketing Manager

The Carlsson Group is looking for a Marketing Manager with relevant qualifications and at least five years' experience in sales and marketing. A competitive salary and generous benefits are available for the right candidate. You must have a good knowledge of current markets, be available to start work at short notice, and must be a good team player. This is a high-powered and fulfilling job for anyone wishing to embark on a career in senior management. The company wishes to fill the vacancy immediately.

applicant		*1–3*	*reasons*
	Kevin Marsh, 21, just left university with a degree in management. Likes working in teams, wants a satisfying job. Unemployed at the moment.		
	Nurdan Ozbek, 35, worked in international marketing for seven years. Degree in Business, used to working under stress and meeting deadlines. One month's notice required in present job.		
	Nuala Riley, 28, six years' experience as editor for a large publisher. Extremely adaptable, excellent relations with colleagues. Three months' notice required.		

30.3 **Match the beginning of each sentence on the left with its ending on the right.**

1 She has set	a presentation to my colleagues.
2 We're making	the minutes at the meeting.
3 I always keep	my phone calls while I took time off.
4 Jane will take	some difficult targets for us all.
5 I have to give	his goals in his career.
6 He never achieved	my appointments.
7 He fielded	preparations for the sales conference.

30.4 **What do the collocations in bold in the text below mean? Use a dictionary to help you.**

Kika started out in a **dead-end job** in a jam factory but she ended up with a **glittering career** on the stage, a **career spanning** five decades. She is quoted as saying 'Stage acting may not be a particularly **lucrative job** but it has to be one of the most **rewarding jobs** in the world.'

31 Business

A Going into business

Interviewer: When did you first **go into business**?

Harris: I **set up a** small **business** selling office supplies in 1989, filing systems, office equipment, that sort of thing. In 1991 I **went into partnership** with my old friend, James Britten. We **made a loss** for the first two years, but then things got better and we've **made a profit** most years ever since. But there have been bad times too.

Interviewer: In what way?

Harris: Well, during the economic recession of the early 1990s, a lot of small **businesses were going under**[1], and I thought our **business would fold**[2], but we survived. All around us, small firms were **going bankrupt**[3]. But in 1994 we **won a contract**, despite **stiff competition**, to supply the local government offices, and that was an important moment for us. We **took on staff** and expanded. And we were proud that we had **created jobs** for local people at a time when unemployment was high. Our **sales figures** improved steadily, and soon we had an **annual turnover**[4] of more than ten million pounds.

Interviewer: So what's the **secret of your success**?

Harris: Well we're quite cautious. For instance, we always **carry out**[5] **market research** before **launching a** new **product**. But also, we **set a high value** on **customer service**, especially **after-sales service**. But at the end of the day, **running a** successful **business** is a combination of hard work, luck and intuition.

Interviewer: Finally, there are rumours that you may **float the company**[6] on the stock market.

Harris: At the moment we have no intention of **going public**[7], and people shouldn't believe everything they read in the newspapers!

[1] failing financially [2] close because of failure
[3] unable to pay debts, so the company's property is sold by order of a court of law
[4] amount of business a company does in a year
[5] the formal equivalent would be **conduct market research**
[6] and [7] start selling shares in a business or company for the first time

B More business collocations

Owing to the economic crisis, many small firms **ceased trading**. [closed their business].
There is **cut-throat competition** in the music industry these days. [very severe competition]
Market forces have caused many factories to close as businesses move overseas. [forces not influenced by government that decide price levels in an economy]
Our local dressmaker has **gone out of business**. People buy ready-made clothes these days.
Her clothes boutique is doing **brisk business** since the shopping centre was renovated.
Business is booming for Internet-based travel companies as more people book travel online. [business is doing extremely well]
She resigned and went to work for a **rival company**.
I **struck/did a deal** with the car salesman and got a 15% discount for cash.
It's quite difficult sometimes to **balance the budget** because of increased costs.
Our company have **put in a bid** for the new leisure centre contract. [offered to do the work for a particular amount of money]

ERROR WARNING Remember, the collocation is **do business**, NOT ~~make~~ business: We're **doing** a lot of **business** in Asia these days.

Exercises

31.1 **Look at A. Complete these collocations.**

1 to .... a company on the stock market
2 to .... a new product
3 to .... a profit
4 to .... bankrupt
5 to .... into business
6 to .... into partnership
7 to .... market research
8 to .... public
9 to .... up a business
10 to .... a loss

31.2 **Match the newspaper headlines 1–6 with the topics of the stories a–f.**

1 **BUSINESS GOES UNDER**
2 **STIFF COMPETITION FOR LOCAL FIRM**
3 **BUSINESS BOOMING IN THE AREA**
4 JACKSON'S STRIKE SUCCESSFUL DEAL WITH JAPAN
5 **ICE CREAM COMPANY TO BE FLOATED**
6 **PAPER COMPANY EXPECTED TO FOLD**

a) a company wins a promising new contract
b) a rival company is causing problems
c) a firm is going to sell shares for the first time
d) a company has ceased trading
e) a company may go out of business
f) local companies' sales figures are looking good

31.3 **Choose the correct collocation.**

1 Our company sets a high *value* / *price* / *cost* on after-sales service.
2 Competition to *earn* / *win* / *achieve* the contract was *strong* / *stiff* / *hard*.
3 You need a wide range of skills in order to *work* / *run* / *go* a successful business.
4 How long have you been *doing* / *making* / *getting* business with China for?
5 The annual *takeover* / *overtake* / *turnover* / *overturn* of our company is growing rapidly.
6 It's my job to *weigh* / *balance* / *add* the budget.
7 We've put in a very competitive *offer* / *bid* / *deal* so I hope we'll get the job.
8 We've been doing *rapid* / *stiff* / *brisk* business all morning.

31.4 **Fill the gaps in this local magazine article.**

Jan Vickers now (1) .... a successful bicycle company in the town. He set it (2) .... ten years ago to cater for students and he has done extremely well. He (3) .... a lot of rental business with the tourist trade at local hotels. In his first year of operations he (4) .... a loss, but his sales (5) .... for his second year showed an upturn and he has never looked back since. Indeed you could say that (6) .... is currently booming as he has just (7) .... an important new contract with a chain of fitness centres. There was stiff (8) .... but Jan (9) .... in a bid which was more attractive than anything that (10) .... companies could offer. So, the deal was (11) .... As a result Jan's company is planning to (12) .... 20 new jobs. When asked to explain the (13) .... of his success, Jan puts it down to his company's emphasis on after-sales (14) ....

FOLLOW UP

Choose an article from the magazine *Management Today*, some of which are available online at www.clickmt.com/public/home/. Make a note of any interesting collocations you find.

Mr Daffy got very few customers after he decided to float his business.

32 Academic writing 1: giving opinions

A Reviewing the work of academics

Look at these extracts from reviews in academic journals.

In 1998, Lucas Georgescu published the results of his **groundbreaking research** on genetics. His latest paper also **makes a significant contribution** to the field. He **sets out** some **powerful arguments** which will **shape**[1] **our thinking** for years to come.

[1] influence

In this latest book, Marina Kass **gives an account of** Karl Marx's philosophy and **provides evidence** to **support the claim** that Garpov seriously misinterpreted Marx. In addition, the book offers a **concise**[2] **summary** of the present state of Marxist philosophy.

[2] short and clear

Partridge **strenuously defends** her theory, which has **come under attack** recently in several journals. She argues that the Prime Minister **played a central role** in the political crisis of 1811, and **goes into great detail** to support her argument.

Nathan Peel attempts to **establish a connection** between mobile phone use and physical damage to users' brains, but he does not offer **irrefutable proof**[3] and the statistics do not show any **significant trends**.

[3] absolute proof, impossible to prove wrong

B Stating things strongly and less strongly

The sentences below express opinions, either strongly or less strongly.

Strong expressions of opinion

The invention of the steam engine was the **key factor** in the birth of the industrial revolution.
The events of 1954 are a **perfect example** of how political leaders make misjudgements that have serious long-term effects.
This is a **clear illustration** of the importance of a strong monetary policy.

Less strong expressions of opinion

The figures offer a **tentative explanation** of the causes of acid rain pollution. [an explanation given by someone who is not totally certain that it is the correct explanation]
The statistics **broadly support** the view that the economy is heading towards recession.

C Other general academic collocations

There is a **strong tendency** in the work of some linguists to suggest that spoken language is inferior to written language.

We must first **gather evidence**, then **carry out** a detailed **study** of all the factors that **play a part** in social conditioning.

You cannot expect your claim to be accepted if you cannot offer **supporting evidence**.

Simon Hart **challenges the theory** of social change put forward by Professor Kemp.

It is important in academic writing always to **acknowledge your sources**. If you fail to do this, you will **commit plagiarism**. [use another person's idea or a part of their work and pretend that it is your own]

ERROR WARNING

We **do research** or **carry out research**, NOT ~~make~~ research.
Someone **puts forward a theory** or **proposes a theory**, NOT ~~gives~~ a theory.

Exercises

32.1 **Look at A and answer the questions.**

1 Which collocations suggest that the writer admires Georgescu's work?
2 Which collocations indicate that Partridge's work has not been accepted by everyone?
3 Which collocations suggest that Marina Kass focuses on facts?
4 Which collocations suggest that Nathan Peel is interested in analysing social statistics?

32.2 **Rewrite each sentence using the word in brackets, so that it keeps the same meaning.**

1 The example of Mrs Brown clearly illustrates the need for better medical services in the area. (ILLUSTRATION)
2 A doctoral thesis must always make it clear where it got its information. (SOURCES)
3 Dr Kahn's results provide clear evidence that our theory is correct. (IRREFUTABLE)
4 The article begins by concisely summarising the background to the research project. (CONCISE)
5 The book interestingly describes the life of Marx as a young man. (ACCOUNT)
6 Janet's theory has been attacked recently in a number of journals. (COME)

32.3 **In B some collocations are presented as expressing an opinion in a strong way. Which collocations in the texts in A also express an opinion in a strong way?**

32.4 **Match the words in the box on the left with the words that they collocate with on the right.**

play	make
set	carry
convinced	go
come	shape

people's thinking	under attack
a contribution	a part
out a study	out an argument
by someone's argument	into detail

32.5 **Choose the correct collocation.**

REVIEWS

Kelly has written a fascinating study of how early people originally got to Australia. He presents some very (1) *powerful / mighty* arguments to support his theory. He offers plenty of (2) *persuading / supporting* evidence to back up his ideas. He has a rather strong (3) *trend / tendency* to (4) *test / challenge* others' theories too aggressively, but in general this is a (5) *groundbreaking / irrefutable* research paper which will (6) *form / shape* thinking for some time to come.

32.6 **Complete this table with collocations for the nouns listed. Use a dictionary to help you if necessary. The first line is completed as an example.**

verb	*adjective*	*noun*
to publish	an outstanding	article
		research
		experiment
		theory
		survey

33 Academic writing 2: structuring an argument

A Organising the text

Here are some useful collocations for organising one's arguments.

Adverbs in English **fall into** two main **categories**: those ending in *–ly* (e.g. *softly*) and those with other endings (e.g. *well*).

Later, I shall **make reference to** the work of Georgi Perelmutter, a leading figure in the field of zoology.

In this chapter, I **draw a distinction between** societies where democracy has developed slowly and those where it came about quickly or suddenly.

Chapter 3 **raises** important **questions** about the need for transport planning in rapidly growing urban environments. It also **touches on issues** such as pollution.

But we also need to **take into consideration** the economic history of Latin America as a whole.

This chapter **makes a case for** re-examining the assassination of President Kennedy in the light of evidence which has emerged since 1963.

B Reinforcing arguments

Look at these extracts from university lectures and note the collocations.

C More collocations for referring to arguments

The book *The Eye of the Universe* **draws an analogy**[1] between the birth of the universe and a lottery. It also **draws parallels**[2] between the formation of new stars and the birth and death of flowers. It **presents the case for** a complete rethinking of how we understand space. The author, Patrick Rivaux, **puts forward the argument** that the universe is as it is because we humans are here looking at it. The author **takes up / adopts the position** that the universe cannot have any beginning or end, and **states** his **opinion** that we can never understand the universe using the human ideas of time and space. He **argues convincingly**[3] that the universe has a unique nature. He **draws attention to** new **research** which **suggests** that other universes may also exist alongside ours. He **briefly summarises**[4] the views of leading physicists and mathematicians, **disagrees profoundly**[5] with some of them and **draws the conclusion** that science alone cannot solve the mystery of the universe.

1 **makes a comparison** between things which have similar features, to help explain an idea
2 says that something is very similar to something else
3 argues in a way that makes people believe that something is true or right
4 expresses the most important ideas in a short and clear form
5 disagrees very strongly or in an extreme way

Exercises

33.1 Look at A and fill the gaps in this article about collocations.

Collocations in English (1) .... into a number of different categories. In this article I should like to draw a (2) .... between 'ordinary' collocations and those that are so fixed that they can be called idioms. Although my main focus is on 'ordinary' collocations, I shall also to some extent (3) .... idioms into consideration too. I plan to (4) .... a number of questions about learning collocations in a foreign or second language. I shall attempt to answer these questions by (5) .... reference to the work of the leading writers in the field. My intention is to make a strong (6) .... for a more intensive focus on collocation in the language learning process. I shall also (7) .... on issues such as pronunciation.

33.2 Look at B and C and complete these collocations.

1 .... the significance of a factor
2 argue something very ....
3 .... an analogy
4 .... support to an argument
5 put .... an argument
6 .... firmly to a belief
7 .... attention to a new trend
8 .... emphasis on one factor
9 disagree .... with someone
10 .... a conclusion

33.3 Choose the correct collocation.

1 This paper *proposes / presents / offers* the case for the complete revision of the theory.
2 Recent research *hints / explains / suggests* that Jackson's theory of economic development is flawed.
3 The author of the book *adopts / adapts / affects* an unusual position on the topic.
4 The writer of the article *explains / states / declares* his opinion very clearly.
5 The article concludes by *briefly / shortly / precisely* summarising the main points that the author wishes to put across.
6 The writer *does / draws / creates* some interesting parallels between life now and life in the Middle Ages.
7 I *keep / take / hold* firmly to my belief in the importance of basic human rights.
8 The book *rises / arises / raises* some key questions but fails to deal with them in a satisfactory manner.

33.4 Correct the nine collocation errors in this review of an academic article.

Kerr takes in a controversial position in his latest article. He gets forward the argument that differences in behaviour between the sexes can be explained totally by the genes. He attempts to do a case for educating boys and girls separately in their primary school years. He argues, occasionally persuadingly, that both sexes would benefit from this. He pulls attention to recent research which, he claims, makes support for his argument. However, he fails to draw a number of important factors into consideration. He also gives no reference to the important work of Potter and Sinclair in this field. I am sure that I will not be alone in disagreeing highly with many of his conclusions.

FOLLOW UP

Look up the words *theory*, *research* and *argument* (with its academic meaning) in a good learner's dictionary. Make a note of any other interesting collocations that you find.

34 Laws and punishments

A Verbs that collocate with law

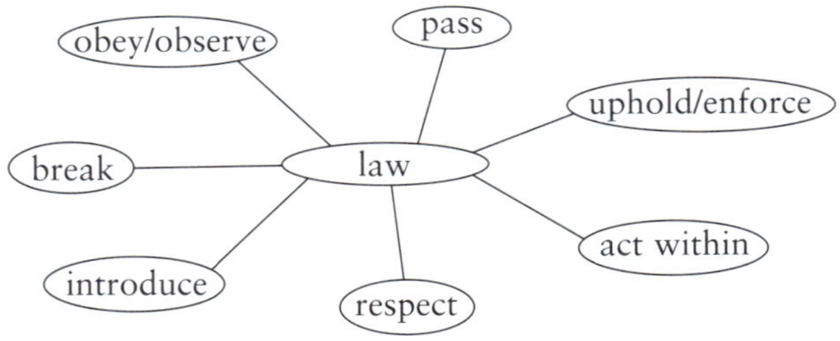

We must all **observe the law** at all times. [formal]
People who refuse to **obey the law** should be punished. [less formal]
A new **law** has been **introduced/passed** forbidding the use of mobile phones while driving.
The company **acted within the law** as regards the rights of its employees. [formal]
It is the job of the police to **uphold/enforce the law**. [make sure that people obey the law]

B Noun and verb collocations

The new **law forbids/prohibits** smoking in all public places. [the law does not allow]
The **rules permit/allow** members to bring guests into the club only at weekends.
These **rules/regulations apply to** all students, not just new ones. [the rules are for]
If we **follow the rules**, at least 20 people must be present at the meeting. [do what the rules say]
The **regulations require/stipulate** that all students must register for the course. [formal: the rules say that]
We have to **comply with the regulations** concerning the testing of equipment. [formal: do what the rules say]
I hope we can **bend the rules** and let her take the exam on another day. [informal: break the rules in a way that is not considered important]

C Punishments

collocation	*example*
carry out an investigation	Police are **carrying out an investigation** into a major theft in a factory in Woodvale.
appear in court	The trial starts today but the witnesses will be **appearing in court** tomorrow.
go on trial	George Arthur Lode, accused of murdering his wife, **went on trial** today.
reach a verdict	The jury are expected to take several days to **reach a verdict**.
a fair trial	It now seems impossible that Harold Graves can receive **a fair trial**, given the media publicity surrounding his case.
be severely punished	That judge believes that all shoplifters should **be severely punished**.
pay/face a heavy fine	People who park on double yellow lines **face a heavy fine**.
face the death penalty	If he is found guilty of murder, he will have to **face the death penalty**.
act as a deterrent	People often support the death penalty because they say it **acts as a deterrent**.
suffer the consequences	Anyone who commits a crime has to **suffer the consequences**.
a harsh penalty/sentence	Some judges are more likely to give **harsh sentences** than others.
a hard legal battle	After a **hard legal battle**, she won compensation for the accident.
win a case	You will need a very good lawyer if you are going to have any hope of **winning your case**.

Exercises

34.1 **Choose the correct verb from A to fill the gaps in this paragraph. Use each verb once only and put it in the correct form.**

In law-abiding societies ordinary citizens are usually happy to (1) .... or (2) .... the law. But there are also rather different societies where most people feel that it is not such a serious matter to (3) .... the law. In such places, people do not seem to (4) .... the law and even the most honest of citizens does not expect always to (5) .... within it. The rulers of such societies have no difficulty in (6) .... or (7) .... new laws but the police have considerable problems when it comes to (8) .... or (9) .... those laws.

34.2 **Match the beginning of each sentence on the left with its ending on the right.**

1 The rules apply	with the regulations.
2 The rules prohibit	to all students in the college.
3 The rules allow students	the rules to allow Mary to submit her coursework a little late.
4 The regulations stipulate	to book college guestrooms at weekends.
5 Most students follow	the use of mobile phones in class.
6 The authorities bent	that coursework must be handed in on time.
7 All students must comply	the rules without too many complaints.

34.3 **Put these events in a crime story in order.**

a) A number of witnesses appear in court.
b) Bill Sikes goes on trial.
c) Bill Sikes is found guilty.
d) Bill Sikes is severely punished.
e) Bill Sikes robs a bank.
f) The jury reaches its verdict.
g) The police carry out an investigation.

34.4 **Answer these questions using one of the collocations from C opposite.**

1 What does every lawyer in a trial hope to do?
2 What does every wrongly accused person who appears in court hope to receive?
3 What do the police do after a major crime is committed?
4 What may happen to people in some countries if they are found guilty of a very serious crime like murder or terrorism?
5 How might the death penalty help to prevent serious crime?
6 What does the jury have to do at the end of a trial?
7 What kind of punishments does a hard-hearted judge give?
8 What kind of fine might a judge impose if the offence is quite serious?

34.5 **Rewrite each sentence using the word in brackets, so that it keeps the same meaning.**

1 Everyone must observe these regulations. (COMPLY)
2 All citizens must obey these rules. (APPLY)
3 The jury found the accused guilty. (REACHED)
4 The police are investigating the bank robbery. (INVESTIGATION)
5 Our company would never break the law. (ACTS)
6 The rules prohibit eating and drinking in the classrooms. (ALLOW STUDENTS)

35 Crime

A Talking about criminals

Note the collocations in these news clips.

The Judge, Mr Newell, said that Hickey was a **hardened criminal**[1] who had **committed** 12 serious **offences**. He ordered that Hickey should **serve a sentence of** at least 15 years in prison.

[1] someone who has committed a lot of crimes

The lawyer for the prosecution, Mr Arthur Larchwood, stated that Henry Banks was already a **convicted criminal**[2] when he was appointed chairman of the company but that nobody knew this fact. He had a **conviction for robbery** dating back to 1986.

[2] someone declared officially in a court of law to be guilty of a crime

The Justice Minister said that the men were not **political prisoners** but were **common criminals**[3] who had committed **acts of terrorism**.

[3] low class criminal, negative term

The judge said it was vital that anyone with a **criminal record**[4] should not be able to get a job where large sums of money were placed in their care. Charles Amworth, 26, had served two years in a prison for **young offenders** ten years ago before working for the bank.

[4] list kept by the police of someone's previous crimes

B Politicians on crime

Politicians often make speeches about crime. Here are some extracts from recent ones.

"In **the fight against** crime we will not just **target serious crime**, but all crime, including **street crime** and **vehicle crime**, so that the streets will be safer for everyone."

"If someone **breaks into your house**, **steals your car**, or **robs you** in the street, then of course you feel society has let you down. That's why we're determined to **tackle crime**."

"We are doing everything in our power to **combat crime**. The **crime rate** has come down, and that is because we have put 10,000 more police officers on the streets and focused on **juvenile crime**[1], because that is where the problem begins."

[1] crime relating to young persons not yet old enough to be considered adults

"This government is doing very little to fight crime. We have all had some experience of the recent **crime wave** in our cities, whether it is **petty crime**[2] or more serious offences."

[2] crime not considered serious when compared with some other crimes

"The **crime figures** are the worst since 1995. We have had a **spate**[3] **of burglaries** in this part of the city, **vehicle theft**, **drug abuse** and so on, and police have reported a **staggering increase** in the number of acts of **mindless vandalism**. It is time the party in power did something."

[3] large number of events, especially unwanted ones, happening at about the same time

ERROR WARNING

Don't forget the difference between *steal* and *rob*. A person **steals *something***, e.g. He stole a car / some money, but **robs *someone*** or ***an institution***, e.g. She robbed an elderly person / a bank. **Steal** is often used in the passive, e.g. My car was stolen.

Exercises

35.1 **Find a collocation in A that matches each definition.**

1 a schoolchild who commits a crime
2 someone who has been found guilty of a crime in a court of law
3 someone who has committed a lot of crimes
4 to spend time in prison as punishment
5 to do something that is against the law
6 someone who is imprisoned for what they believe
7 someone who has committed a crime (a disapproving term)
8 a document stating that someone has been found guilty in a court of law.

35.2 **Match the headlines from a local newspaper with the first lines of their stories.**

1 JUVENILE CRIME RISING

2 DRUG ABUSE SCANDAL

3 PETTY CRIME CONTINUES

4 POLICE TARGET VEHICLE THEFT

5 PENSIONER ROBBED

6 CRIME FIGURES OUT TODAY

a) 80-year-old Marianne Roberts had her house broken into and some money and jewellery stolen while she was asleep in front of the TV last night.
b) An increasing number of young people are getting involved in criminal activity according to a report published yesterday.
c) So many cars have recently been stolen in the city that the police are launching a special campaign to tackle the problem.
d) A detailed report on crime in the UK is to be published later today.
e) Small-scale robberies remain a significant problem in this area and police are concerned that the problem may soon become more serious.
f) A number of TV celebrities have been named as having attended a party where illegal drugs were being openly used.

35.3 **Fill in the gaps in this paragraph.**

Police are concerned about the growing number of offences that are being (1) .... by young people in our town. They say that increasing numbers of youngsters are (2) .... into people's houses or (3) .... their cars. Indeed, police claim that it is probably young (4) .... who are to blame for the recent (5) .... of burglaries in our town. Police are proposing a special campaign to (6) .... the problem and are asking for the public's support in this (7) .... against (8) .... crime.

35.4 **Answer these questions.**

1 Would you feel pleased or worried if there were reports of a crime wave in your area?
2 What sorts of crime might be considered as petty crime?
3 If the police are *targeting* serious crime, what are they doing?
4 What word could replace *tackle* in this sentence? *The police are doing all they can to tackle petty crime in the city centre.*
5 What does the phrase *an act of terrorism* mean?
6 Which of these words could complete the phrase *a spate of …: robberies, young offenders, drug abuse?*
7 Give an example of mindless vandalism.

36 News

A Collocations about newspapers

collocation	*example*
a (news) story breaks	The singer was out of the country when the **story** about his wife **broke**.
news comes in	TV newscaster: **News** has just **come in** of an earthquake.
news leaks out	Although the two stars tried to keep their relationship secret, **news** of it soon **leaked out**.
hit the headlines	The scandal is expected to **hit the headlines** tomorrow.
make headlines	A dramatic story like that will **make headlines** world-wide.
front-page headline	The scandal was the **front-page headline** in all the newspapers.
the latest news	**The latest news** from the earthquake zone is more hopeful.
be headline/front-page news	Any story about the Royal Family will **be headline/front-page news** in Britain.
item of news	The main **item of news** today is the earthquake in Broskva City.
run a story [publish a story]	The *Daily Times* recently **ran a story** about an affair between a famous rock star and a politician.
flick through the newspaper	He **flicked through the newspaper** as he didn't have time to read it properly.

B The language of news stories

MINISTER **GIVES THE GO-AHEAD** TO PLANS

In a surprising **turn of events** last night, the government agreed to plans for the development of the City. **Interested parties**[1] will **hold talks** throughout the week.

[1] people or groups who have a connection with a particular situation, event, etc.

MINISTER QUITS

The Arts Minister has resigned after only six months in the **top job**. He has **attracted attention** over his **controversial decision** to re-introduce charges for museum entry.

PEACE TALKS END IN FAILURE

Peace **talks** between the Eastern Liberation Army and the government of Karavia **broke down** last night. Civil war is now likely.

ANTI-SMOKING CAMPAIGN

The Minister for Health today **outlined plans** for a national anti-smoking campaign. The government intends to **launch the campaign** in the new year.

TOURIST TAKEN CAPTIVE

A tourist was **taken hostage** when rebel troops **seized control** of St Pips Airport last night. The government has **lost control of** the area. Our reporter in St Pips is **keeping a close watch on** the situation and we shall be **keeping you informed** as the **news develops**.

LIGHTNING STRIKES

A building **caught fire** when **lightning struck** a farm in Hampshire yesterday. Fortunately there was **no loss of life**.

ERROR WARNING

Note that we say **the latest news**, NOT the ~~last~~ news.

Exercises

36.1 Complete the collocations in these descriptions of TV programmes. 'Pick of the week' means 'most highly recommended programmes for the week'.

	Our pick of the week
Monday **7.00–7.30pm BBC1**	The .... news from the world solo balloon attempt in this 30-minute documentary with live pictures from the balloon.
Tuesday **8.15–9.00pm ITV2**	Through the Window: a unique look at the private residences of the celebrities who .... headlines around the world.
Wednesday **10.25–11.25pm DTV**	Last year, rock star Izzy Arbuttle was .... news. But where is he now? Jo Prees investigates the star who became a very private person.
Thursday **8.00–8.45pm KTV3**	When news .... out that singer Millie Logan was seeking a divorce from Hal Daker, no one believed it. Millie tells her own story.
Friday **9.15–9.55pm MBC**	The Deenazon drug scandal which .... the headlines last year left 10,000 people with health problems. A major newspaper .... a story claiming that scientists had not done proper tests. But who was to blame?
Saturday **6.30–7pm QSRTV**	The famine in Geura was the ....-.............................. headline on every major newspaper last year. But what is life like for the people of Geura now?
Sunday **5.30–6.30pm LAK3**	Next Sunday, European Heads of State will .... a news conference to end their summit. It could contain important developments.

36.2 Complete the crossword.

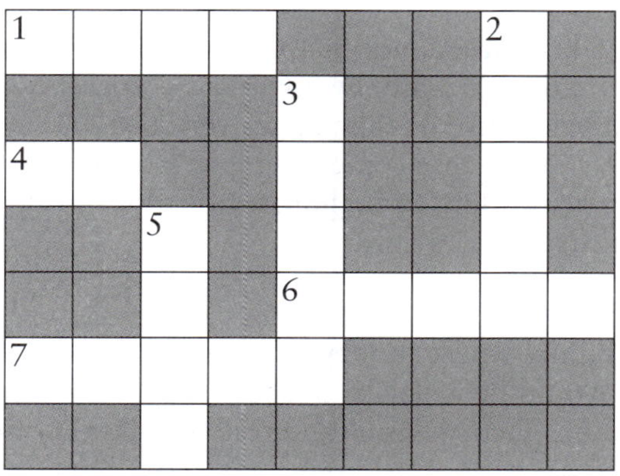

Across

1 The parties could not agree and the talks broke ....

4 The plan got the ....-ahead yesterday.

6 We must keep a .... watch on the dollar-euro exchange rate.

7 Big news stories do this.

Down

2 The Minister outlined .... for a new university funding system.

3 I don't really read the newspaper, I usually just .... through it.

5 There was an interesting news .... in the local paper yesterday.

36.3 Complete the collocations.

1 In a horrific .... of events, ten people who were taken hostage have been murdered in cold blood. We will .... you informed as more news .... in.

2 Rebel troops .... control of the capital of Jalamaa last night. Meanwhile, five police officers were .... captive by rebels in the south of the country.

3 Lightning .... a house yesterday which immediately .... fire.

4 The government will .... talks with all .... parties to try to end the strike.

5 Charles Ankram is to quit the .... job of personal adviser to the President. He recently objected to a .... decision to cut next year's health budget.

6 The government has .... a campaign to clean up the countryside.

37 Money

A Spending money

Here are some verbs which often collocate with money.

collocation	*meaning*	*example*
spend money (on)	give money as payment for something	Juan **spends** a lot of **money** on travelling.
save money	keep money for use in the future	We're **saving** a little **money** each month to buy a new car next year.
waste/squander money (on)	spend money in a bad way; *squander* is stronger and is only used about large sums of money	Sara **wasted/squandered** all her **money** on clothes and fast cars.
change money	exchange one currency for another, e.g. dollars for euros	You can **change** some **money** at the airport.
throw money around	spend money in an obvious and careless way on unnecessary things	If Jim keeps on **throwing** his **money around** like that, he soon won't have any left.
throw money at	spend a lot of money, possibly more than necessary, trying to solve a problem	The government think they can solve the problem by **throwing money at it**.
donate money (to)	give money to help society in some way	The business **donates** a lot of **money** each year to charity.

B Prices

Many collocations including the word **price** are connected with height. **Prices** can be **high** or **low**. If they are very low, they may be called (usually by advertisers) **rock-bottom prices**. **Prices** may **increase**, **prices go up** and **prices rise**. If they go up very fast we say that **prices soar**. Occasionally **prices go down**. If you say that something is **reasonably priced**, you think it is neither too cheap nor too expensive. Calling something a **ridiculous price** may mean it is much too cheap or much too expensive.

C Getting money

Henry and his brother grew up in a family where **money was always tight**[1]. Henry hoped that when he was grown-up, money would be never be **in short supply** for him. Henry's brother only wanted a **steady income** but Henry wasn't interested in just **earning a good salary**, he wanted to make **big money**[2], to be **seriously rich**[3]. He started **making money** at school when he sold the sandwiches his mother had made him to other children. He also worked in his school holidays to **earn money**. He put this money in a bank account and hardly ever **made a withdrawal**[4] from it. When he left school, he **raised enough money** through the bank to buy his first shop. He **got a really good deal**[5] because he found a shop that was **going cheap**[6]. By the time he was twenty he had already **made a small fortune**[7] though, of course, most of his **money was tied up**[8] **in** his business.

1 there wasn't much money
2 informal: a lot of money
3 informal: very rich
4 took money out of the bank
5 informal: got a bargain
6 informal: selling for a low price
7 made a large amount of money
8 not available for spending because it was needed for his business

Exercises

37.1 **Read these remarks by different people, then answer the questions.**

Briony: I sent 100 euros to the Children's Fund for the Developing World.
Philip: I won 100,000 dollars on the lottery and bought stupid, useless things. I have almost nothing left now.
Anthony: I went into the bank with 1,000 euros and came out with the equivalent in Australian dollars.
Marianne: The garden was in a terrible mess after the storm. I paid a gardener a lot of money to sort it out but he didn't seem to make it any better.
Catherine: I put 5,000 euros in an account which gives 4% interest.

	name
1 Who threw money at something?	
2 Who saved money?	
3 Who donated money?	
4 Who squandered money?	
5 Who changed money?	

37.2 **Complete these sentences using collocations from B opposite. Use each collocation once only.**

1 In March 1998, computer chip prices were around 150 dollars. In September 1998 they were 850 dollars. In just six months prices had ....
2 An airline is offering a return flight from London to New York for just 50 dollars. At first sight this seems like a ...., as many people on the same flight will be paying 1,000 dollars or more.
3 Given that most first-class hotels were charging 300 dollars a night because of the festival, at 275 dollars our four-star hotel seemed ....
4 Hand-held computers are now selling at .... prices because there's so much competition. One that cost 250 dollars a year ago now costs only 70.
5 Car prices .... down last year, but they will probably .... again before the end of the year as steel becomes more expensive.

37.3 **Choose the correct collocation.**

1 Bank assistant: Can I help you, Madam?
Customer: Yes. I'd like to *take / get / make* a withdrawal from my account please.

2 Bank Manager: Is your company *getting / making / taking* money?
Business customer: Yes. We are in profit. So I have a *firm / steady / strong* income.

3 Teenage son: Dad, will you lend me money to buy a car?
Father: Well, money is rather *slim / hard / tight* at the moment. Ask your mother.

4 Jake: These cameras aren't as expensive as I thought.
Fran: That's because they use film. They're *going / asking / giving* cheap right now because everyone is buying digital cameras, which are ridiculously expensive because they are in such *low / short / little* supply.

5 George: We need to *bring up / rise / raise* money for the new club house. Any ideas?
Joe: Well, we could have a children's sports day and get all the parents to contribute.

6 Mick: You must have made a *slight / slim / small* fortune when you sold your house.
Kathy: Yes, I did, but the money is all *closed up / tied up / packed up* in the new one.

7 Oscar: I guess Zara is making *big / large / huge* money with her Internet business.
Erica: Oh yes, she's *absolutely / utterly / seriously* rich now.

38 War and peace

A War

When **war broke out**[1], my grandfather **joined the army**. **War was declared** on his 25th birthday. He didn't want to **go to war** but he had no choice. The government were sending troops to the south where they expected **fierce fighting**. At first there were just **minor incidents** but soon it developed into **all-out war**[2]. My grandfather has told me how terrified he was the first time he came **within firing range**[3] of the enemy. They saw him and **opened fire**[4] but he was able to escape. A couple of his friends, though, were killed or **taken prisoner**. After several months our **army went into action** in the first **decisive battle** of the war. The **battle raged**[5] for several days. My grandfather said he hated being involved in **fighting the war** and that the only armies we should have should be **peacekeeping forces**. He can never forget **the horrors of war**, and he believes that we must do everything we can to **avert**[6] **war** in the future. I agree.

1 suddenly started
2 a complete/total war
3 the distance within which the enemy could hit him by firing their guns
4 started shooting
5 the battle was very violent
6 prevent something bad from happening

B Peace

collocation	*example*
bring about peace	It will be no easy task to **bring about peace** in the area.
negotiate a peace agreement	It can be useful to invite a neutral country to help **negotiate a peace agreement**.
call a truce/ceasefire	Although **a ceasefire has been called** for the duration of the peace negotiations, hopes of its success are not high.
sign a (peace) treaty	At the end of the war, all the countries involved **signed a peace treaty** in Paris.
lasting peace	Hopes for a **lasting peace** are, unfortunately, fading fast.
peace activist	**Peace activists** around the world staged a series of massive demonstrations against the war.
keep the peace	After the war was over, UN troops were sent into the troubled area to help **keep the peace** there.
restore order	Soldiers were sent in to **restore order** after the uprising.

C War expressions in everyday language

The police fought a **running battle** with football hooligans in the town centre.

The people of the village **put up a heroic fight against** the construction of the new motorway, but finally **lost the battle**.

The bank robbers didn't **offer** any **resistance** when the police surrounded them.

The President is **fighting for his life** tonight in the City hospital after a major operation.

TIP Some collocations connected with war and military action are also used in a business or political context, e.g. a **price war**, to **fight crime**, a **war on crime**.

Exercises

38.1 **Use a word from the box in the correct form to complete the extracts from news broadcasts.**

go horrors join avert fight open rage

1 The president said he is ready to .... to war against Collocania. He said he had done everything possible to .... war, but now there was no alternative.

2 A two hour battle .... in the Raguni district today after troops .... fire on rebel positions.

3 The army will continue to .... the war against the drug barons.

4 The president said that young persons who .... the army must expect to fight to defend their country. They would experience the .... of war, but they must be brave.

38.2 **Rewrite the sentences, replacing the words in brackets with collocations from the opposite page.**

1 The war between Adverbia and Collocania (started) in 1983 after a dispute over territory in the northern province. At first there were just (small events) but it soon turned into (a full-scale war). The war ended after (a battle which finally decided the course of events) in 1987.
2 There was (very violent fighting) in the capital city yesterday. United Nations (forces who will maintain peace) are expected to enter the city as soon as (the armies say they will stop firing at each other).
3 Forces sent in to (make the peace continue) in the troubled region of Phrasalia had to (turn back) after they came (within the firing distance) of rebel artillery.
4 The Sornak Republic today (officially stated that it was at war) against Hobrania.
5 Armed troops were sent in to (bring order again) after the riots and violence of last week.
6 Even though the two sides (put their names to a document officially stating that the war was at an end) last July, fighting has started again and hopes for (a peace which might continue for a long time) are fading.
7 As more of our soldiers were killed or (captured and put in prison), (people who were actively promoting peace) organised demonstrations against the unpopular war.
8 Representatives of the two sides are meeting in Zurich in an attempt to (make peace) in the troubled region. It is hoped that they will (have negotiations and agree the details for peace) which both governments can accept.

38.3 **Correct the collocation errors in these sentences.**

1 The police fought a walking battle with a group of violent demonstrators.
2 I feel we are missing the battle to persuade the management to increase our salaries.
3 The students made up a heroic fight against the plan to increase course fees.
4 I was surprised that the Management Committee sent no resistance to our demands.
5 A tiny baby with a rare heart condition is fighting his life in the General Hospital tonight.

38.4 **Use your dictionary to find two more collocations for each of these words.**

army soldier battle weapon to fight peace

FOLLOW UP Look at the Peace section of the United Nations website – www.un.org/peace/. Make a note of any interesting collocations that you find there.

39 Global problems

A The environment

Look at these extracts from letters to an international magazine.

> Your article on **climate change** was excellent. **Rising sea levels** and the increase in **greenhouse gases**[1] are the result of our actions. We are **disturbing the ecological balance** everywhere, as can be seen in the decrease in **fish stocks**[2] in the oceans.

[1] gases which cause the greenhouse effect, especially carbon dioxide
[2] the number of fish

> It is clear that we must **tackle pollution** before it is too late. **Exhaust fumes** from millions of vehicles and the burning of **fossil fuels**[3] are causing **irreparable**[4] **damage** to our environment.

[3] fuels such as gas, coal and oil
[4] which cannot be repaired (also *irreversible*)

> We must accept that we have seriously **depleted**[5] **the ozone layer** in the last few decades by our selfish actions. Embracing **green politics** may be our best hope in the long term, but we need urgent short-term measures too.

[5] reduced something in size or amount, especially supplies of energy, money, etc.

> **Crops fail** year after year in some of the poorest parts of the world. This has brought **devastating**[6] **famines** to some regions and equally **devastating floods** to others. We call these **natural disasters**, but it is human beings who are causing them.

[6] causing a lot of damage or destruction

B Poverty

Look at this radio interview with Pascal Delrio, an international expert, talking about poverty.

Interviewer: Mr Delrio, do you believe we can solve the problem of world poverty?

Delrio: I am more optimistic now than before. Millions of people have succeeded in **escaping poverty** in the last decade, but it is also true that in some regions, more people than ever are living **below the poverty line**, and we must help these people to **lift them out of poverty**.

Interviewer: But how can we achieve that?

Delrio: I accept that there is no **simple solution**. The **widening gulf**[1] between rich and poor in some countries is often due to external forces beyond their control. Some of the most **deprived regions** have large populations living on the **margins of society**, and it is for these specific groups that we can do most.

Interviewer: But poverty is not just an issue for **developing countries**, is it? We have thousands **sleeping rough**[2] every night in cities like London and New York, and **street children** in a lot of big cities around the world.

Delrio: I agree, and I accept that children and adults who **live on the streets** are in **desperate need**, and that these social conditions **breed crime**. But so much depends on **the global economy**. Right now, we have a **golden opportunity** to **combat poverty**. Perhaps we cannot **eradicate**[3] **poverty** altogether, but we can certainly **alleviate**[4] **poverty**, and that is our challenge.

Interviewer: Mr Delrio, thank you very much.

[1] an important difference between the ideas, opinions, or situations of two groups of people
[2] in the open, without shelter [3] get rid of completely [4] make less serious

C Other global problems

Thousands of people seek **political asylum** in other countries every year. Most are genuine **asylum seekers**, but some are **economic migrants** looking for a better life.
Hundreds of people **took to the streets** to demonstrate about third-world **debt repayments**.
A terrible **earthquake hit** the region last year. The **death toll** was massive.
The **sexual exploitation** of children is a **world-wide problem**, as is **child labour**.

Exercises

39.1 Complete the collocations.

1 a rise in the number of asylum ....
2 to deplete the ozone ....
3 bad social conditions .... crime
4 increasing amounts of greenhouse ....
5 a golden .... to combat poverty
6 people who .... rough
7 a massive .... toll
8 to be in desperate ....
9 to .... people out of poverty
10 below the poverty ....

39.2 Match sentences 1–5 with sentences a–e.

1 There was a big protest against child labour.
2 There is new evidence of a widening gulf between the wealthy and more deprived sectors of society.
3 There has been some small success in tackling marine pollution.
4 The problem of street children in big cities has become a global crisis.
5 A spokesperson for one of the biggest charities said access for economic migrants should be made easier.

a) There is some evidence to suggest that fish stocks are beginning to rise slightly in the North Sea.
b) People wanting to come to this country to escape poverty should be welcomed.
c) Large numbers of people took to the streets yesterday to demonstrate against the increasing employment of children in appalling conditions.
d) A worldwide study of young people who sleep rough has raised universal alarm.
e) Figures published today indicate that the divide between the rich and the poor is getting bigger.

39.3 Fill in the gaps in this announcement.

Environment Concern is a new magazine for people interested in (1) .... politics. The first issue includes an article on what happened to local crops when the earthquake (2) .... Santa Graziela last year. Another feature looks at the problems which (3) .... repayments are causing for (4) .... countries and how this affects people who live on the (5) .... of society there. We appreciate that there is no simple (6) .... to the problem of poverty in today's world but we have asked four experts what *they* would do to (7) .... poverty. Their answers make stimulating reading.

39.4 Answer these questions about the collocations in A.

1 What will happen if crops fail in an important agricultural area?
2 Name two fossil fuels.
3 Name three types of natural disaster.
4 What might a devastating flood do to an area?
5 What could governments do in response to a devastating famine?
6 What are green politics concerned with?
7 What is the cause of rising sea-levels?
8 Why are exhaust fumes an increasing problem?

FOLLOW UP

There are many articles on global problems in the *New Internationalist* magazine. Choose one from their website (www.newint.org/) and note any interesting collocations that you find. The magazine also has special articles written in an easy style for learners of English. Go to its *Teaching Global Issues* page.

40 Time

A Collocations using the word *time*

collocation	*example*	*comment*
spend time	I **spent some time** in South America when I was younger.	NOT ~~passed~~ in this context – though you can say things like *reading* ***passes the time***.
waste time, save time	Don't do it like that. You're **wasting time**. You'll **save time** if you do it like this.	*Spend*, *waste* and *save* are often used with *money* as well as *time*.
tell someone the time	Can you **tell me the time**, please? I left my watch at home.	NOT tell the ~~hour~~
free/spare time	What do you like to do in your **free/ spare time**?	Both expressions refer to the time when you are not working.
have time to	I'm sorry, I didn't **have time to** do my homework.	Compare: Jo **doesn't have time for** lazy people. [has no patience with]
make time for	The doctor's very busy but he'll try to **make time for** you.	*Make* here has a simple meaning of *create*.
kill time	We got to the airport very early, so we had a meal in the restaurant to **kill** (some) **time**.	to fill in the time while you are waiting to do something you have planned
take your time	No need to hurry – you can **take your time**.	This means you can be as long as you wish.
bang/dead/right on time	The train left **bang/dead/right on time**.	Exactly on time – the first two are very informal.

Here are some other useful expressions relating to time.
We **had a good/great time** at the party. [NOT ~~spent~~ a great time]
Jayanthi **had the time of her life** in Brazil.
Your attitude to work may change a bit as **time goes by** / as **time passes.**
I couldn't finish the exam because I **ran out of time.**
You'll be sorry **big time** for speaking to me like that! [informal: extremely]

B Past and future

The **past few weeks** have been really difficult for Tina's two grown-up children. They're both at university writing dissertations. Her son's is on **early 21st century** fiction while her daughter's is about life in **prehistoric times** – she's not interested in the **recent past** at all. They are both working very hard. They are nearly finished but there are lots of last-minute things left to do. They **set their alarms** for five o'clock and get up as soon as the **alarm goes off.** They work **from dawn till dusk**[1] and indeed sometimes they stay up until **the small hours**[2]. Tina can't wait until they stop working such **ungodly hours**[3]. It's **taking them ages** to complete their work but Tina is sure it will eventually all be **worth their while**[4]. She is sure they both **have a great future ahead** of them. She thinks they will both get good academic jobs **in the not too distant future.** Of course, no one can know what **the future holds,** but I hope she is right.

[1] all day
[2] 2, 3, 4 am
[3] unreasonably late or early hours
[4] worth the time spent

Exercises

40.1 Complete the collocations in these advertisements for leisure activities.

What do you do when you're not working? If you want to spend your (1) .... **time** in pleasant, relaxing surroundings, why not (2) .... **some time** at the Haven Health Centre? Slow down, (3) .... **your time.** (4) .... **time** for yourself in your busy world.

Don't (6) .... **time** writing appointments on your calendar! You can (7) .... valuable **time** by using Timemate, the new software from Compcorpus. Just enter appointment details and Timemate will automatically text you on your mobile phone to remind you. You'll arrive (8) .... **on time** for every appointment and never be late again.

Comchess

If you like chess, you'll love this. Chess for your laptop or hand-held computer. Great for (5) .... **time** on a long plane or train journey! Play with a friend or play the machine. Visit our website and order online: www.comchesswld.com

Can you (9) .... **me the time,** please? How often do people ask you this and you can't answer? Never again! Just press the 'time' button on the new Boza mobile phone and the correct time is yours!

40.2 Correct the collocation errors in these sentences.

1 I was hoping to finish my dissertation last year but I ran off time.
2 It's hard work learning a language but I'm sure you'll find it's worth the while.
3 Les spends all this time at the office – he's there from dusk till dawn.
4 As a teacher I often wonder what the future has for my pupils.
5 Did you spend a good time on holiday?
6 I didn't have time for doing the ironing last night.

40.3 Complete the second part of each conversation with a collocation using the words in brackets.

1 Adam: Don't forget, everybody. We have to get up at 5a.m. tomorrow.
Sally: Well, we'd better all .... (ALARMS)

2 Ahmed: Did you enjoy your trip to Malaysia?
Inez: Yes. It was fantastic. I had .... (LIFE)

3 Judith: I think as you get older you change your attitude towards your parents.
Mark: Yes, I think you learn to respect them more as .... (BY)

4 Hugh: You must come and visit us some time. Don't keep putting it off.
Mary: Yes. I'll try to come and see you in the .... (NOT/DISTANT)

5 Ruth: You were late for work this morning!
Andy: Yes. I didn't wake up. The alarm didn't .... (OFF)

6 Willis: Sonia was studying till 2 a.m. again last night.
Teresa: Yes, she always stays up working until .... (SMALL)

40.4 Find two collocations for each of these words in your dictionary.

day hour clock minute

41 Sound

A Sounds in nature

Look at these extracts from short stories.

At first there was an **eerie**[1] **silence**, then there was a **rumble of thunder** in the distance. Soon **the wind** was **whistling** through the trees and we could hear **the waves crashing** on the beach. The storm had begun.

[1] strange in a frightening and mysterious way

It was a lovely place for a picnic. There was a little **babbling**[2] **stream** and **birds were singing** in the trees. Then we heard **the patter of rain** on the leaves above us. Sadly, it was turning into a typical British summer's day.

[2] low, continuous noise of water flowing over stones

No sound **broke the silence** of the wintry landscape. Then suddenly **two shots rang out** and we heard the **piercing**[3] **cry** of a dying bird. The hunting season had begun.

[3] high, loud and unpleasant

B Everyday sounds

collocation		*example*
deafening, ear-splitting	sound, noise (used as a countable noun)	We heard the **ear-splitting/deafening sound/noise** of three huge military aircraft passing low over our heads.
excessive	noise (used uncountably)	People who make **excessive noise** after 10 p.m. are very antisocial.
background	noise	When you work in a big office you get used to constant **background noise**.
muffled[1]	sound	We could hear the **muffled sound** of music from the flat above us.
shrill[2]	voice, laugh	Marie has such a **shrill voice**. I can't listen to her for long.
raucous[3]	laughter	I could hear **raucous laughter** coming from the party next door.
dull	thud	The heavy box fell off the shelf on to the carpet with a **dull thud**.
grating[4]	noise, sound	The big old iron door made a **grating noise** as it opened.
loud/almighty	bang, explosion	Suddenly there was a **loud** / an **almighty bang**, the lights went out and smoked poured from the back of the TV set.
roar	traffic	I couldn't sleep with the constant **roar** of the **traffic** outside my window.
music/radio	blare (out)	Loud **music** was **blaring out** of the radio in the kitchen.
machine	hum[5], whirr[6]	As we talked to the factory owner, the **machines hummed/whirred** in the background.

[1] made quieter/or less clear (e.g. by the walls)
[2] loud, high sound that is unpleasant or painful to listen to
[3] loud and unpleasant
[4] harsh, unpleasant sound
[5] make a continuous low sound
[6] make a low, soft, continuous sound

C Verbs and sounds

A person can **give a sigh, a laugh, a loud cry, a cry of pain/surprise/alarm, a gasp, a groan.**
A person, animal or thing can **make a scratching/clicking/rustling/crackling sound.**

Exercises

41.1 **Look at A. Choose the correct collocation.**

My friends and I went camping this weekend. We put up our tent in a lovely spot beside a (1) *babbling / whistling* stream. The birds were (2) *piercing / singing* and it felt great to be so far from the noisy traffic of the town. The weather wasn't very good but it was cosy listening to the (3) *rumble / patter* of rain on the roof of the tent. When it eventually stopped there was (4) *an eerie / a piercing* silence all around us. The silence was suddenly (5) *broken / closed* when a shot (6) *crashed / rang* out. Someone was shooting rabbits.

41.2 **Are these noises loud or soft? Write L (loud) or S (soft) after each collocation.**

1 a deafening sound
2 a dull thud
3 music blaring out
4 a machine whirring
5 raucous laughter
6 a shrill voice
7 an almighty bang
8 an ear-splitting noise
9 a machine humming
10 someone giving a sigh
11 leaves making a rustling sound
12 a muffled sound

41.3 **Match each statement 1–8 with a response a–h.**

1 I think those people might have had too much to drink.
2 Did the group react negatively to the news that the flight was delayed?
3 Our neighbours really make excessive noise, I think.
4 I hate it when chalk makes that horrible noise on the board.
5 I think this wonderful weather is going to change soon.
6 It's a comfortable hotel but it's a bit noisy, isn't it?
7 Did you hear that almighty bang in the middle of the night?
8 Did the child react when she had the injection?

a Yes, it really is too much to play such loud music after midnight.
b Yes, I thought I heard a rumble of thunder in the distance.
c Yes, she gave a cry of pain.
d Yes, the roar of the traffic kept me awake most of the night.
e Yes, you can tell by their raucous laughter.
f Yes, I was woken by what sounded like a loud explosion.
g Yes, they all gave a groan of disappointment.
h Yes, it's a horrible grating sound, isn't it?

41.4 **Answer these questions.**

1 What is more likely to make a dull thud – a person falling out of bed onto a carpeted floor in the room above you or a heavy metal box falling onto a stone floor?
2 Who is more likely to have shrill voices – primary schoolchildren or old age pensioners?
3 If waves are crashing on the beach, are they more likely to be little waves or big waves?
4 If you hear a piercing cry, is it more likely to be from a machine or from a bird?
5 What is more likely to make an ear-splitting noise – a group of motorbikes roaring past or a large waterfall in a fast-running river?

42 Distance and size

A Distance

collocation	*example*
a considerable/long/short distance from	The hotel is a **considerable distance** from the beach. [quite a long way]
within commuting/ walking distance	We have to live **within commuting distance** of my husband's office. [where it is possible to travel to work every day]
cover/travel (a distance of) x kilometres	On our cycling tour we managed to **cover (a distance of)** about 40 **kilometres** a day.
far-off/far-flung places	Bill is always travelling to **far-off/far-flung places**. [distant]
at close range	I've never seen a member of the royal family **at** such **close range** before. [so near]
neighbouring town/ country/area	Many people who work here actually live in **neighbouring towns**.

B *Little, small* and *large*

We talk about **low prices, low wages, low levels.** (NOT ~~small~~)
We say **small quantities, small numbers, small amounts, a small increase.** (NOT ~~little~~)
The opposite is **large quantities, large numbers, large amounts, a large increase.** Similarly, we talk about problems or objects being **on a large scale** or **on a small scale**:
If you are walking in the mountains you need **a large scale map.**
The UK has similar problems to the USA, but **on a smaller scale.**

In informal spoken English we often use **little** after another adjective to make it sound more friendly, e.g. **poor little** Joe, **dear little** dog, **nice little** room.

Little can also mean young, e.g. **little brother** [informal: younger brother, NOT ~~small~~ brother; the opposite is **big brother**]. Sometimes **little** or **small** suggests that something is not very important, e.g. a **little problem,** I've got a lot of **little things** to do, to make someone **look small,** to **make small talk** [talk socially, about unimportant subjects].

C Other size collocations

We can talk about **fat books** and **slim books** as well as **fat people** and **slim people.** Only **people** (not books) can be **plump** or **skinny** or **painfully thin.**

We use **a great deal of** (NOT ~~large~~ or ~~big~~) in contexts like this:
She should be able to help you because she has **a great deal of time / a great deal of money / a great deal of energy / a great deal of enthusiasm.**

Major and **minor** often collocate with words relating to problems or points in an argument, e.g. **major/minor difference, major/minor change, major/minor effect, major/minor difficulty, major/minor point, major/minor issues, major/minor factor.**

ERROR WARNING Take care with the different collocations that go with *tall* and *high*. We talk about **tall people, tall trees, tall buildings,** but **high mountains, high prices, high interest rates, high heels, high tide, high jump.** Make a note of any collocations with *tall* or *high* as you notice them.

Exercises

42.1 **Look at A and complete the collocations in these short travel texts.**

1 Tassia, and the n.............................. towns of Hiol and Gebja, were all damaged during the civil war but have been rebuilt.

2 The roads in Baxa are bad, so don't expect to .... more than 50 or 60 miles in a day. Petrol stations tend to be a c.............................. distance from one another, so watch your fuel level.

3 If you love heading for ....-flung destinations in far-.............................. places, but in the safety of a small group, then Safetrek Holidays could be what you are looking for.

4 Within .... distance of our hotel was the Alfama Bird sanctuary, where we were able to see a wonderful variety of birds at .... range.

42.2 **Cross out the five collocation errors in this text and write the correct words in the right-hand column. The first one has been done for you.**

Although we had a ~~little~~ increase in our pay	......small......
last month, we still earn very small wages.	....
We have not had a big deal of help from the	....
union, and tall prices mean that life is not	....
easy. Luckily, we only have a small level of	....
inflation at the moment.	

42.3 **Change the underlined words so that each sentence has the *opposite* meaning.**

1 Cilla is having some <u>minor</u> difficulties at work.
2 She was wearing red boots with <u>low</u> heels.
3 The company manufactures these components on a <u>small</u> scale.
4 We have had <u>low</u> interest rates for the last three years.
5 It's quite a <u>fat</u> book.
6 There were <u>small</u> quantities of oil in the tanks.
7 I had to share a room with my <u>big</u> brother until I was ten.
8 Jane is <u>shorter</u> than her mother.

42.4 **Answer the questions.**

1 What adverb beginning with 'p' collocates with thin?
2 Do we normally say 'a plump book'?
3 What do we call the maximum level of the sea on a beach or in a harbour?
4 Which adjective usually collocates with people, trees and buildings: *high* or *tall*?
5 Which word could fill the gap? That poor .... child looks lost.
6 Which word could fill the gap? Dave has a great .... of enthusiasm.
7 Which word could fill the gap? I'm no good at making .... talk.
8 Would we say 'Could you help me do some small things before dinner?'
9 If you owe the bank money, what kind of interest rates do you prefer?

43 Colour and light

A Describing colours

Look at these letters to *Home making* magazine, asking for advice about colours.

I love **bright** colours. I have a **bright yellow** jacket and I think the **colour goes well with** my bright green trousers. But my best friend thinks the **colours clash.** She says I should get some **yellow trousers to match the jacket.** Who is right?
K. Williams (Mrs)

With black jeans the **colour** always **fades** after two or three washes. Is there any way to stop this?

A. Lacey (Ms)

I put a pair of red socks in the washing machine with my white shirt and my **pale**[1] **blue** shorts and the **colour ran.**
E. Jitt (Mr)

My clothes are so dull, and I always wear **subdued**[2] **colours.** My favourite is **dark green.** How can I add a **touch of colour** to my wardrobe without spending too much money?
B. Grey (Mr)

[1] a light colour that is not bright or strong

[2] not very bright

B Describing light

Look at these extracts from short stories, where the writers describe different kinds of light.

It had **grown dark**, the **candle flickered** and Bertram could see almost nothing, but suddenly a powerful **beam of light** shone into the room and a police officer entered, with a torch in her hand.

A **ray of sunlight** fell on his face and woke him up. It was six a.m. Soon the **glare of the sun** would make it difficult to see his way across the desert. He must get to the village at once.

It was **pitch dark** when she left the house, but by the time she arrived at the beach, the **faint glow** of dawn was visible on the horizon. The sky was **tinged with gold**.

Above her, the **stars twinkled** in the night sky. Then she saw a **pinpoint of light** in the distance. As she walked towards it she realised it was a man on a bicycle coming towards her.

C Colour and light: metaphorical collocations

The law about re-using pictures from the Internet seems to be **a grey area.** [an unclear area]
The trip to Brazil certainly **added colour** to our rather boring lives.
My brother cares a lot about **green issues** and has volunteered to do conservation work.
The government tried to **blacken his name** because he was critical of their policies. [destroy his reputation]
I'm hoping Hilary can **shed/throw some light on** what happened at work yesterday. [explain]
My sister's illness **cast a shadow over** our New Year family reunion. [made it less happy/cheerful]
Jim has always **been under the shadow of** his super-intelligent sister. [got less attention]

Exercises

43.1 **Look at A and choose the right collocation to complete each of these sentences.**

1 Shocking pink, lime green and orange are very .... and I personally prefer to wear more ....
2 I think I'll wear my dark blue sweater and those grey trousers. The .... well together.
3 When I washed my red and white football shirt, the .... and it's ruined now!
4 I don't think it is a good idea to wear a purple top with orange trousers and red shoes – the .... terribly, in my opinion.
5 I like that red brooch on your black dress – it adds a lovely .... - ....
6 My son always washes new jeans so that the .... before he wears them.

43.2 **Match the two halves of each collocation.**

1 a candle	dark
2 a beam	glow
3 pitch	area
4 a faint	someone's name
5 a star	of light
6 pale	a shadow
7 green	green
8 a grey	flickers
9 cast	twinkles
10 blacken	issues

43.3 **Rewrite each sentence using the word in brackets, so that it keeps the same meaning.**

1 The police are looking for someone who can explain how the accident happened. (SHED)
2 He has always been in an inferior position to his world-famous father. (SHADOW)
3 In the east the sky had some golden shades in it. (TINGE)
4 Joe's crazy behaviour certainly brightens up our dull office. (COLOUR)
5 Very bright sun can make driving difficult at this time of day. (GLARE)
6 She walked until the fire was just a little light in the distance. (PINPOINT)
7 Darkness was falling and Jill began to feel a little afraid. (GROWING)
8 The newspapers seem to be trying to destroy the minister's reputation. (BLACKEN)

43.4 **Now answer these questions about the collocations in exercise 43.2**

1 What probably causes a candle to flicker?
2 A *beam* of light is often used about the headlights of a car or the light of a torch. What similar phrase is used about sunlight?
3 Would you use *pitch black* to describe someone's hair or the night?
4 If you see a light as *a faint glow* is it likely to be far away or near to you?
5 What is the difference in meaning between saying that a star *shines* and a star *twinkles*?
6 What kind of issues are green issues?
7 What do you feel about something if you say that it is a grey area?
8 What sort of thing might cast a shadow over a special celebration?
9 If Mark accuses Karen of 'blackening his name', what has Karen done?
10 If something adds colour to someone's life or to a story, what happens to the life or the story?

44 Texture

A Adjectives and their opposites for describing textures

adjective + noun	*opposite adjective + noun*	*example*
dry hair	greasy hair	You need to wash **greasy hair** more often than you need to wash **dry hair**.
dry skin	oily skin	This cream is good for **dry skin** – that one would be better for **oily skin**.
smooth skin, surface, complexion	rough skin, surface, complexion	Use this cream and the **rough skin** on your hands will soon become **smooth**.
smooth water, sea	choppy or rough water, sea	I hope the **sea** will be **smooth** today – I hate **rough seas**.
smooth road, flight	bumpy road, flight	The outward **flight** was very **bumpy**. I hope the return **flight** is **smoother**.
soft pillow, bed, ground	hard or firm pillow, bed, ground	I'd much rather sleep with a **firm pillow** than a very **soft pillow**.
tender meat	tough meat	It's deliciously **tender meat** – how did you cook it? My steak is always **tough**.
sharp pencil, knife	blunt pencil, knife	This **pencil's blunt** – I can't work unless I have a good **sharp pencil**.

B Verbs relating to textures

When the temperature gets warmer, **ice melts** but **snow melts** or **snow thaws**.

As time goes by, **fruit goes soft** and **bread goes hard**.

A **voice softens** or **hardens** [gets more friendly or gets less friendly] and an **attitude softens** or **hardens**. [gets less severe or gets more severe]

C Other texture words with their collocations

[1] You can paint your walls using either **matt paint** or **gloss paint**. Gloss paint and gloss photos have a shinier finish than matt. [2] cut into small pieces, opposite would be **coarsely chopped** [3] large grains of salt rather than small or **fine grains**

D Metaphorical uses of texture words

If things **go smoothly**, they go well.

If someone **has a sharp tongue**, they say unkind things.

If you're in a difficult position, you can say that you're in a **sticky situation**. [informal]

Coarse jokes are vulgar jokes, jokes in bad taste.

Velvety sky is dark and deep with a beautiful soft smooth quality like the cloth velvet.

Exercises

44.1 **Can you remember the pairs of adjectives at A on the opposite page? Change the underlined words to their opposite meaning.**

1 I always prefer to sleep on a soft pillow. How about you?
2 My grandmother had very rough skin, which surprised me as a child.
3 Remember the Parazo restaurant? It was where we had the really tender lamb chops.
4 I found an old sharp penknife in the pocket of a jacket I hadn't worn for years.
5 The surface of the lake was very rough as we set out on our fishing trip.
6 Can you help me? I'm looking for a shampoo for dry hair.
7 I've always had rather dry skin, so I always use Milona face cream.
8 We had a smooth flight over the mountains.

44.2 **Use collocations from the opposite page to complete the second speakers' answers.**

1 Customer: (*In a photo-lab*) Is there a choice of finish for the prints?
Assistant: Yes. You can either have .... or ....

2 Roger: The temperature was minus five yesterday; it's plus eight today!
Nelly: Yes. And the ice on the lake has already ....

3 Hilda: What's that loaf of bread like now? It's about four days old.
Bill: I'm afraid it has ....

4 Tim: I think the protesters are very angry about this new road, and getting angrier.
Elana: Yes, I think attitudes ....

5 Sheila: There are some oranges in the bowl, but I'm afraid they may be old.
Kate: Mm. Yes. They are rather old. They're beginning ....

44.3 **Complete the crossword.**

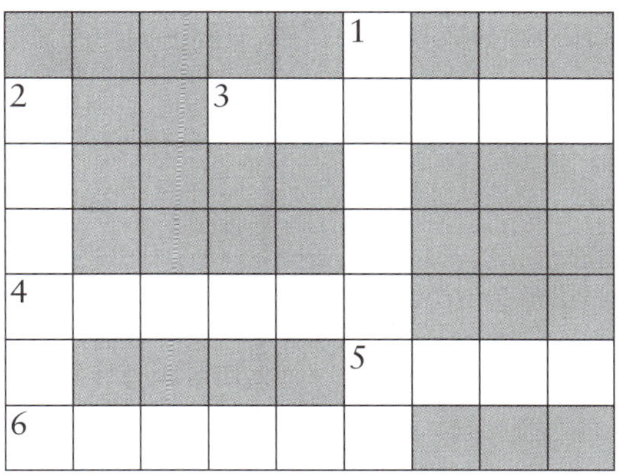

Across
3 the texture of yogurt
4 the texture of large grains of sand
5 It's warm; the snow's beginning to ....
6 The little child had .... fingers after eating chocolate.

Down
1 adjective meaning 'has a beautiful soft, smooth quality or appearance, usually dark or deep'
2 The couple spoke very angrily at first, but their .... softened when they realised it was a mistake.

44.4 **Find four collocations on the opposite page that have positive associations and four that have negative associations.**

FOLLOW UP Find more collocations describing texture in English language magazine articles or advertisements about beauty and health products, or about fabrics and furnishings.

45 Taste and smell

A Food and restaurant reviews

Look at these descriptions of smells and tastes in travel review articles.

Everywhere you go, the **fragrant perfume** of Caranza Island's wild flowers follows you. And in the village of Jarca, the **distinctive aroma**[1] of the local dishes and the **smell** of fresh coffee **wafting**[2] across the square from the small cafés is simply wonderful.

[1] a slightly literary word used to refer to pleasant smells (often of food and drink, e.g. coffee); often used with adjectives such as *distinctive*, *rich*, *strong*, *sweet*, *appetising*

[2] moving gently through the air

For many people, octopus is **an acquired taste**[3], but it's a must on the south coast, and the **subtle**[4] **flavour** of the local vegetable, *quingat*, provides a perfect accompaniment. The **fresh scent** of herbs is everywhere in the local markets.

[3] something you dislike at first but start to like after trying it several times

[4] not noticeable or obvious

B Negative collocations connected with smells and tastes

I can't drink **bitter coffee**. I'll have to put some sugar in this.

There was nothing in the fridge except an old carton of **milk** which had **gone sour**.

The lovely beach was completely spoilt by the **acrid**[1] **smoke** and **noxious**[2] **fumes** from a **foul-smelling chemical factory** nearby. [[1]strong smelling, causing a burning feeling in your throat [2]poisonous]

Body odour can be extremely unpleasant and embarrassing. [an unpleasant smell on a person's body that is caused by sweat]

C More taste and smell collocations

Ray: Jane, do you think this cheese is bad? It has a **strong smell**. **Have a taste**, tell me what you think.
Jane: Hmm. Let me **have a smell** ... mm ... When did you buy it? It **smells off**[1] to me.

[1] no longer fresh or good to eat because of being too old

Tania: There was an **overpowering stink** coming from the river today as I drove over the bridge. It always **gives off a smell** in the hot weather but this was dreadful.
Mick: Yes, I passed there the other day. It's a **revolting stench**[2]. The pollution is getting worse and worse.

[2] *Stench* is a stronger, more extreme word than *stink*. *Revolting* means extremely unpleasant, disgusting.

Chris: Do I detect a **whiff**[3] **of perfume**? Are you meeting someone special tonight?
Rita: It's none of your business!

[3] slight smell

D Smell and taste: metaphorical collocations

Her cruel remarks **left a bad/unpleasant taste in our mouths**. [left an unpleasant memory]
I **tasted freedom** when I gave up my job and travelled for a year. Now I can't go back to normal life.
Bob and I **share the same taste in** music; we often buy the same CDs.
She has **developed a taste for** fast cars. She's just bought a bright red Ferrari.
We **smelt danger** and decided not to enter the city. It was a wise choice.
I didn't hear every word, but I **got the flavour of** what he was saying and I didn't like it.

Exercises

45.1 Look at A. Match the beginning of each sentence with its ending.

1 I think caviar must be an acquired	fumes from the factory behind it.
2 The delicious aroma of fresh coffee	is just too bitter for my taste.
3 The park was spoilt by the noxious	wafted in from the kitchen.
4 We just loved the fragrant	smoke from the bonfire.
5 I particularly enjoy the subtle	taste – I don't like it very much.
6 Smell the bottle and tell me if the milk	perfume of the blossom on the trees.
7 I usually love coffee but this coffee	is sour or OK to drink still.
8 It must be the wet wood causing such acrid	flavours that herbs give to food.

45.2 Divide the collocations in the box into those that have a positive meaning and those that have negative connotations.

acrid smoke   appetising aroma   foul-smelling chemicals   fragrant perfume
noxious fumes   overpowering stink   revolting stench   fresh scent

positive	*negative*

45.3 Read the sentences and answer the questions about them.

1 *Greg has developed a taste for visiting old churches.*
How frequently do you think Greg visits old churches?

2 *Greta always leaves a whiff of perfume behind her.*
Does Greta leave a strong smell or a light one?
Is it a pleasant or an unpleasant smell?

3 *As I entered the train carriage I couldn't help noticing the body odour.*
Does the speaker notice the smell of sweat or the smell of cosmetics?

4 *Jim asked his girlfriend to have a taste of the sauce he was preparing.*
Does the girlfriend probably take a lot or a little of the sauce?

5 *Some fish were rotting in a bucket and were giving off an overpowering stink.*
Did the speaker like the smell?
If the speaker had said *revolting stench* instead of *overpowering stink*, would this have made the smell seem better or worse?

6 *If you just read the introduction to the article, you can get the flavour of it.*
How could you say *get the flavour* in a different way?

7 *The argument has left an unpleasant taste in my mouth.*
Is the speaker upset by something he has eaten or something that has happened?

8 *Hilary and I get on so well together because we share the same taste in lots of things.*
Do Hilary and the speaker only like the same kinds of food or other things too?

FOLLOW UP Look up the words *taste, flavour, aroma, smell, perfume, scent* and *odour* in a good learner's dictionary. Make a note of what kinds of things they collocate with.

46 Number and frequency

A Commenting on how much or how many

These adjectives collocate strongly with both *number* and *amount*. Try to use them instead of *small* or *large* where appropriate.

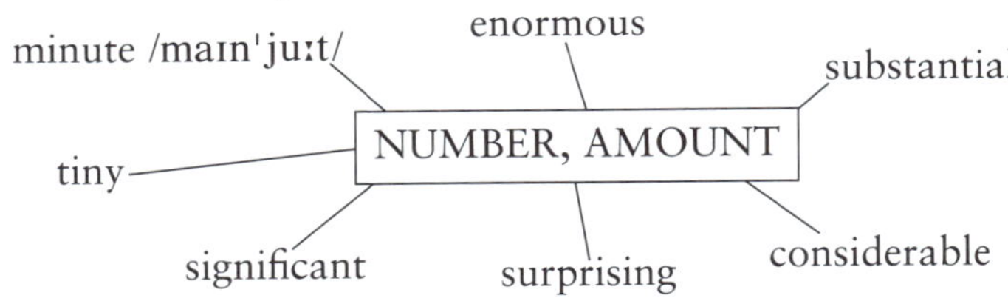

B Talking about numbers

collocation	*example*	*comments*
odd/even numbers	51 is an **odd number** – 50 is an **even number**	odd numbers = 1,3, 5 etc. even numbers = 2, 4, 6 etc.
a decline/drop in the number of	There's been a recent **decline in the number of** boys joining the army.	*Drop* is more informal than *decline*.
an increase/rise in the number of	The **increase in the number of** homeless people is worrying.	*Rise* is slightly more informal than *increase*.
come to a total of	If we add up all the figures it **comes to a total of** 794.	A calculation **comes to a total of** x; the person calculating **arrives at a total of** x.
birth rate rises/falls	Over the last few years the **birth rate has been falling**.	A **rate** can also **drop** or **decline** as well as fall.
a unit of currency/ measurement	The standard **unit of currency** in most EU countries is the euro.	We also talk about a **unit of electricity**, **unit of length**.

C Frequency

Widespread [existing or happening in many places or among people] collocates strongly with a lot of words relating to either attitude (**widespread interest, widespread support**) or problems (**widespread damage, widespread poverty**):
There has been **widespread support** for the government's new policy on education.
The heavy winds at the weekend have caused **widespread damage.**

Rare [infrequent and special] collocates with things in the natural world (**rare disease, rare bird, rare species**) and also with collectable items of special interest (**rare stamps**).

If someone repeatedly does something that annoys you, you can use the expression **keeps asking, keeps interrupting, keeps hitting**, etc. This is common in informal spoken English:
Please don't **keep interrupting** me when I'm trying to work.
The children **keep asking** me when we're going to buy a new computer.

Constant and **continual** also convey the idea of something happening repeatedly:
I couldn't get on with my work today because of **constant interruptions** – the phone kept ringing every five minutes.
It was a mistake to go on holiday with them. Their **continual complaining** drove us mad.

D Describing graphs and charts

Profits **rose sharply/steeply** in July, but **fell sharply/steeply** in September.
There was a **dramatic rise/fall** in the number of students applying to university this year.
Numbers of mature students have **increased steadily/gradually** since the 1960s.
The number of crimes committed in the city has **remained constant/stable** since 2001.

Exercises

46.1 Use adjectives from A opposite instead of the underlined words to complete the collocations.

1 I only put a very small amount of chilli in the soup but it was still too hot for some people.
2 There was an extremely large amount of information to read, 5,000 pages, which was far too much for one person to absorb.
3 We can't ignore the fact that a small but important number of people disagree with the plan.
4 There was an unexpected number of people at the meeting who had never voted in their lives.
5 The government's new budget will mean that a rather large number of people will have to pay more in taxes. (Give two answers.)

46.2 Choose the correct collocation.

1 17, 29 and 395 are all *strange / odd / unequal* numbers.
2 Many European countries use the euro as their standard unit of *money / value / currency*.
3 26, 8 and 192 are all *equal / level / even* numbers.
4 The bill *comes / arrives / gets* to a total of 287 dollars.
5 The unemployment rate is *falling / decreasing / lowering*.

46.3 Use words from the box to complete the news reports. You may use the words more than once.

decline	rare	keep	widespread	drop	fall	rise

Following (1) .... criticism of the government's environmental policy and a recent report showing a (2) .... in the numbers of seabirds along the nation's coastline, a scheme has been announced which, it is hoped, will result in a (3) .... in the population of birds, especially of those (4) .... species which are seriously threatened with extinction.

Unfortunately, last year's storms did (5) .... damage to homes in the north, and the damage is still visible in many places. One local resident complained 'We (6) .... asking the authorities when we will be compensated. They (7) .... promising to sort it out but then nothing happens.' There has been a steady (8) .... in the number of severe storms in the area, with an average of two per year recorded in the 1980s and more than five per year now.

Although only a relatively small number of people die from (9) .... diseases each year, a plan to build a research centre into such diseases has received (10) .... support from all political parties. 'I'm glad to say that we have seen a steady (11) .... in the incidence of these diseases,' a medical expert said. 'But we must be careful. The numbers could (12) .... again if we do not continue to support research.'

46.4 Write sentences describing the sales figures in the chart. Use all the collocations from D.

Sales of mobile phones

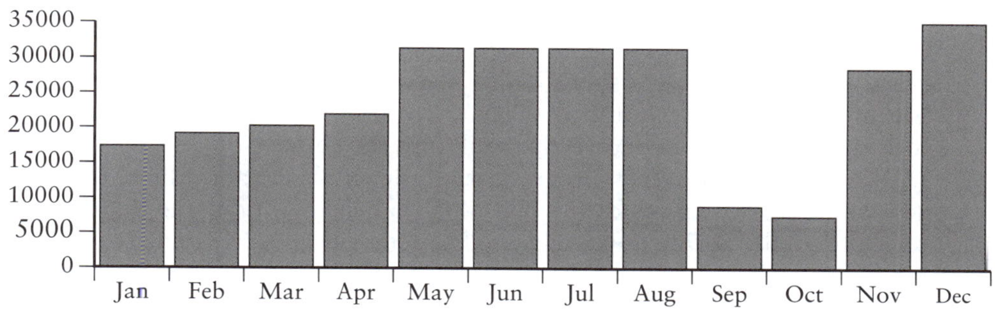

47 Movement and speed

A Synonyms of *fast*

adjective	*collocations*	*examples*
fast	car, train, lane, computer, pace	The **fast train** to London only takes 45 minutes. I don't like driving in the **fast lane** on the motorway.
quick	look, glance, answer, decision, shower, lunch	We had a **quick glance** at the menu and went in. I think I'll have a **quick shower** before going out.
rapid*	growth, decline, change, progress, increase, movement	There has been a **rapid decline** in the number of sea-birds visiting the island each year. The builders made **rapid progress** with the new stadium.
speedy*	recovery, conclusion, response, access	She made a **speedy recovery** after her operation. The new web pages provide **speedy access** to airline and train timetables for 52 countries.
swift*	action, response, reaction, recovery	The government took **swift action** to change the law. This is an extremely urgent matter. I hope you will be able to give us a **swift response**.
prompt*	payment, reply, response	**Prompt payment** of bills is a good idea. I was happy that my letter received such a **prompt reply**.
brisk	walk, pace, business, efficiency	We had a **brisk walk** before lunch. She does everything with **brisk efficiency**.
hasty	decision, exit, conclusion, words	We should not make **a hasty decision**; we may regret it later. He made a **hasty exit** when he saw his wife enter the room.

* these are more formal

Note also these collocations with speed:
This car has a **top speed** of 180 kilometres per hour. [maximum speed]
He drove **at breakneck speed** along the motorway and was soon stopped by the police. [carelessly fast and dangerous]

B Slow movement and stopping

It was fascinating to see the winning goal again **in slow motion**.
We were stuck in **slow-moving traffic** for an hour on our way to the airport.
After the accident the traffic **slowed to a crawl** and then finally **came to a standstill**.
He always does everything **in an unhurried manner**. [slow; implies slight criticism]
We got up late and had a **leisurely breakfast**. [done in a relaxed way, without hurrying]
I'm trying to learn the violin, but my progress is **painfully slow**.

C Changes in speed, movement and direction

As it left the city, the train **gathered/picked up speed** and headed north.

We **took a shortcut** through a narrow side-street and saved ourselves a 15-minute walk.
Several roads were closed, so we had to **make/take a detour**. [a different or indirect route]
I **lost my balance** and fell off my bike.
I **lost my footing** and fell down the bank into the river.
I tried to **steer the conversation** away from my terrible exam results. [change the subject]
She **took** a few **steps** towards the bus, then changed her mind and decided not to go after all.
I **turned** my bike **upside down** and tried to repair it.
One of the packages I posted **went astray** and never arrived. [got lost]

Exercises

47.1 **Look at A. Choose the correct collocation.**

1 Joe gave Lynne a *speedy / fast / quick* glance to see if she was OK.
2 If you come to a *hasty / prompt / brisk* decision, it may well be the wrong one.
3 I marked my e-mail as urgent so I hope I get a *brisk / prompt / rapid* response.
4 The missile attacks provoked a *fast / swift / hasty* reaction from the other side.
5 There has been a *fast / rapid / quick* increase in the number of tourists visiting the city since the museum was opened.
6 Luke has a passion for *quick / swift / fast* cars.
7 I'm glad to say that business has been very *brisk / prompt / swift* all morning.
8 I think I'd better bring the meeting to a *brisk / speedy / fast* conclusion now, as we are running out of time.

47.2 **Fill in the missing words in this paragraph about a day out.**

Last Saturday we put our bikes on the train and had a lovely day out. At first the train moved along slowly, but as we reached more open countryside it soon (1) p.............................. up speed and after about an hour we had reached our destination, a small town at the foot of the mountains. We took our bikes and got off the train. We were surprised to find a lot of slow-(2) m.............................. traffic in the town and indeed after a few minutes the traffic actually came to a (3) s............................... There was a festival on in the main square. Fortunately, as we were on bikes we were able to (4) m.............................. a detour through some back lanes. Eventually we were on a steep road leading to the mountains. I'm not as fit as I should be and cycling uphill was (5) p.............................. slow but it was worth it. Near the top we got off our bikes and had a (6) l.............................. picnic, enjoying the magnificent views. After lunch, I got up and (7) t.............................. a couple of steps back to take some photos. I (8) l.............................. my footing and fell. Fortunately, I didn't hurt myself. Cycling downhill was much easier, though at one point I (9) l.............................. my balance and fell off my bike. We had a drink at a café in the valley beside a little river. We then (10) t.............................. a shortcut across a field and got back to the station in time for the train home.

47.3 **Correct the collocation errors in these sentences.**

1 Let's take the speedy train to Paris even though it's more expensive.
2 Jack did his best to drive the conversation away from the topic of work.
3 If you take the clock upside down, you might find the maker's name on the bottom.
4 You could only be sure which runner had won the race by watching the film of the finish in slow movement.
5 I posted your birthday present in plenty of time. I hope it won't get astray.
6 Let's have a rapid lunch and then get back to work as soon as possible.
7 Charlie always does everything in an unhurrying manner.
8 The car was travelling at neckbreak speed through the residential streets.
9 She bought a motorbike with a peak speed of almost 200 kilometres per hour.

48 Change

A Ways of talking about change

Small changes

I **made** a few **adjustments** to the gears and my bike works much better now.
We've had to **make a slight alteration** to our plans for the evening.
We've **made** a few **modifications** to the software so that it suits our systems better.
We've decided to **adopt** a new **approach** to the parking problem.
I've lost some weight – I need to **have** some of my **clothes altered**.

Major changes

It is often much more difficult than you'd expect to **break a habit.**
The organisation helps alcoholics who want to **kick the habit.** [informal]
The Internet has **revolutionised the way** people do research.
Her grandparents **converted to Christianity** in the last century.
Yoga has **the power to transform** the way we feel. [make a positive change]

B Other collocations with *change*

collocation	*example*
change places/seats	Would you like to **change places/seats** with me – then you can sit next to your friend.
change jobs/schools/doctors, but move house NOT ~~change~~ house	Jack is going to **change jobs** next year so they'll have to **move house** and the children will have to **change schools**.
change your mind	Harry is planning to study law at university but he may **change his mind**.
change the subject	Whenever Fiona talks about marriage, Bill **changes the subject**.
change the beds	I'll get some clean sheets and we'll **change the beds**.
change the baby	It's your turn to **change the baby** – there's a packet of nappies upstairs.
change your clothes	Do you want to **change your clothes** before we go out?

Note that *exchange* cannot be used in any of the collocations in the box. You **exchange money** (from one currency to another), **exchange addresses** (when people give each other details of where they live), **exchange ideas** (when people share their thoughts about something).

C Some error warnings

Here are some collocations relating to the theme of change which seem to cause particular problems, so note them carefully.

Some new jobs will **become available** soon. (NOT ~~get~~)
I'm sure George will **become successful** one day. (NOT ~~get~~)
The **standard of living is rising** steadily / **is improving**. (NOT ~~increasing~~ or ~~growing~~)
Interest in old cars has **grown** considerably over the last few years. (NOT has ~~increased~~)
There's been a big **improvement in** your **performance** this year. (NOT ~~increase~~)
A number of **problems arose** during the journey. (NOT ~~appeared~~)

ERROR WARNING

Something **rises**, for example, **prices rise**, **profits rise**, **the sun rises**. But you **raise** something. You **raise** (NOT ~~rise~~) **your hand**, the government **raises** (NOT ~~rises~~) **taxes**, and during a meeting you sometimes **raise** (NOT ~~rise~~) **a question**.

Exercises

48.1 Complete the collocations in these work e-mails between Chris and Elaine.

Hi Elaine,
I've (1) .... a couple of modifications to the schedule for the sales conference. I know we've always done it the same old way, but think we should (2) .... the habit this year and try a new format. See the attachment. What do you think?
Chris

Chris,
I'm worried about these changes, especially losing the coffee break. Lots of us are addicted to our coffee break and couldn't kick the (3) .... if we tried. I'm sure if you just (4) .... a few minor adjustments or a (5) .... alteration to the timetable here and there it would be fine, but big changes like this will be unpopular!
Elaine

Hi again Elaine,
Thanks for your comments. I wasn't trying to revolutionise the (6) .... we do things, but I do think we should (7) .... a new approach. The sales conference is serious work, not an excuse for time off. But let's think about it.
Chris

48.2 What would you say? Use collocations with *change* from B opposite.

1 A friend starts to talk about something unpleasant and you would prefer to talk about something else.
YOU: I'd rather not talk about that. Let's ....
2 You are on a train, sitting next to the window. A parent and child get on and the child sits next to you. Offer the child your window seat.
YOU: Would you like ....?
3 You order something in a restaurant but immediately wish you had ordered something different. You call the waiter back.
YOU: Sorry, I've .... Can I have fish instead?
4 A friend says she hates her job and is bored with it. Suggest she gets a new one.
YOU: Have you thought about ....?
5 You and a friend are wearing smart clothes and are about to do a messy, dirty job. Suggest you put different clothes on.
YOU: It's going to be messy. I think we should .... before we start.
6 You have three guests coming to stay. Suggest to your housemate that you should put new sheets on the guest beds.
YOU: They're arriving this evening. We should ....

48.3 Choose the correct collocation.

1 The standard of living has *grown / risen / increased* in the last ten years.
2 We *changed / exchanged / passed* some interesting ideas with our colleagues in the USA.
3 Tom and Jo are *changing / transferring / moving* house to be nearer Jo's elderly parents.
4 The new model of this computer will *become / get / make* available in September.
5 At the end of the presentation we could *raise / rise / arise* any issues that we wanted to discuss.
6 The firm *got / made / became* very successful, but then problems *appeared / arrived / arose*.

49 Ways of speaking

A Wedding speech

Whenever I **make a speech** I always try to **get to the point** as quickly as possible. I could **tell** a lot of **stories** about Jim, my best friend since childhood, but I don't want to embarrass him, so I won't. Also, before the wedding, I **gave** him **my word** that I wouldn't **crack** any **jokes**, as I'm really bad at **telling jokes.** So I'll do no more than **wish** Jim and Sandra **luck** and hope they have a long and happy life together.

B Business conversation

Paula: David, I wonder if I could have a **brief chat** with you about our new secretary?

David: Mm. Yes. I had a **quick word** with Lorna about it yesterday; she said there have been problems.

Paula: Could we talk now? I know it's a **delicate subject** but I don't think we need to make it a **lengthy discussion** with everyone involved.

David: Well, actually, I'm rather glad you **raised the subject**. Yes, let's talk.

Paula: Well, **speaking off the record**[1], every time you **give** her **instructions**, she never seems to understand, and if you **challenge** her **directly** she just **pleads ignorance**[2]. The other secretaries are **complaining bitterly** that they end up doing her work. One of them **dropped a hint** that she might resign if nothing is done about it. I could tell by **the tone of her voice** that she was serious.

David: Oh dear. Oh well, I'll **have a word** with her and **make it clear** that she has to improve or we may have to ask her to leave.

Paula: Thanks, David. Anyway, let's **change the subject**. How's the sales plan going?

David: Oh, not bad, but I have to **tell** you **the truth,** I've been very busy with other things lately. In fact I was going to **ask** you **a favour** …

Paula: I know what you're about to say! Don't worry, I'll help you with it.

[1] saying something you do not want to be publicly reported
[2] says she does not know about something

C Problem page

Dear Aunt Cloda,
I find it difficult to **get into conversation** with new people, or to **join in a conversation** that's already started. And even if I do talk to someone, I feel as if I'm boring them. I like meeting people and I want to be able to get to know them and not just **make polite conversation**. What can I do?
Nora Peepoutova

Dear Aunt Cloda,
A friend of mine **made an** interesting **observation** the other day: she said I always **address** people too **politely** and I **apologise** too **profusely** if I do something wrong. Why am I like this? Why can't I relax and be informal?
Al Loof

Dear Aunt Cloda,
I was at a party recently and I heard my friend Margie **strike up**[1] **a conversation** with a handsome man sitting next to her. Then, after a while, during a **lull**[2] **in the conversation**, I heard her **whisper softly** to him that she was not married. She is. Why did she **tell a lie**? Should I have told him?
Gel Luss

[1] start
[2] quiet period

ERROR WARNING

We **speak** a (foreign) language. We don't say 'I can ~~talk~~ Arabic/French/etc.'

Exercises

49.1 Replace the underlined words with a collocation from A.

1 I always get a bit nervous whenever I have to speak in public.
2 Julia promised me she would not leave the country without informing me.
3 I wish Fred would hurry up and get to the important part of what he's trying to say.
4 I hope that you will be successful in your new job.
5 After dinner everyone sat around sharing funny stories.

49.2 Correct the collocation errors in these sentences.

1 You can borrow my camera – I'll make you instructions about how to use it.
2 I could say you a lot of stories about what we used to do when we were kids.
3 That's enough about computers. I think it's time we moved the subject, don't you?
4 On the train I hit up a conversation with an interesting man from Japan.
5 I can't talk Japanese.
6 I'm afraid I really don't have time for a large discussion on the matter.
7 The US President George Washington is famous for confessing after saying a lie.
8 I don't like your note of voice – there's no need to be so aggressive.

49.3 Complete this e-mail.

Hi, Jim,

Any chance we could have a brief (1) .... before the meeting this afternoon? I'd like to have a (2) .... word with you about the third item on the agenda. I want to (3) .... you a favour. It's rather a (4) .... subject, so I won't put anything in writing just now. And when we do get together, I'll be speaking strictly off the (5) ...., of course. I'll (6) .... everything clear when we meet – so look forward to (7) .... a word with you soon.

See you soon,

Bob

49.4 Complete each sentence with a word or phrase from the box.

bitterly	conversation	enough hints	ignorance	in the conversation	observations
politely	profusely	softly	the conversation	the subject	the truth

1 I hope you will always tell me ....
2 I wish you had never raised ....
3 I hope she'll get the point if I drop ....
4 You can usually rely on Jack to make some interesting ....
5 I don't believe George when he pleads ....
6 I was too shy to join in ....
7 When he arrived late he apologised ....
8 When I give my students a lot of homework, they always complain ....
9 It doesn't sound quite natural to address your fellow students so ....
10 'I love you,' he whispered to her ....
11 I'll try to attract his attention during a lull ....
12 It's not always easy making polite ....

50 Ways of walking

A Key walking collocations

Cathy always preferred **to go** places **on foot** rather than driving. She loved **going for a walk** in the park in the early morning. There were always a surprising number of people around. Some were **taking a stroll** with their dogs, while more energetic people chose to **go jogging**. Cathy liked **going running** too, but she preferred to **go for a run** in the evenings. In the morning she liked a **brisk walk**. Today she was surprised to see a man **pacing up and down** beside the lake. He was **taking** long **steps** as if he was measuring the length of the lake. Cathy was puzzled but thought little more of it at the time.

B Adjectives and adverbs associated with walking

collocation	*example*	*comment*
an easy / a gentle walk	It's an **easy walk** into town from here.	**Gentle walk** suggests going slowly; **easy walk** suggests it's neither long nor difficult.
heavy/light steps	I could hear his **heavy steps** coming down the corridor.	*Heavy* can suggest either that the person walking is large or that they are sad, angry or tired.
a leisurely/gentle stroll	We can go for a **leisurely stroll** around the park later.	**Go for a stroll** is more common in speech than **take a stroll**.
to walk briskly/ swiftly	The nurse **walked briskly** over to the bed.	Use these adverbs sometimes instead of *quickly*.
to pick your way cautiously	She **picked her way cautiously** along the icy pavement.	= walked carefully across a dangerous or difficult area
to wander aimlessly	I didn't know what to do so I just **wandered aimlessly** around town all morning.	Both *wander* and *aimlessly* suggest having no particular purpose.
to stride angrily/ confidently/ purposefully	The president **strode confidently** across the room.	We can also say also **took confident/ angry/purposeful strides**. *Striding* suggests large steps.

C Walking through life

Walking collocations are often used metaphorically. Notice the examples in this text.

Jack always did very well at school. He **walked**[1] every **exam** he ever went in for. His teachers used to call him a **walking encyclopaedia**. It was only when he left school that he began to **run into problems**. He couldn't decide what job to choose. Many **different walks of life** appealed to him. He didn't want to **rush headlong into**[2] something that he would later regret. Eventually he decided he most wanted to become a writer. The next day he **took his first faltering steps**[3] at writing a novel. After only a month or two he had **made great strides**[4] and was ready to take his book to a publishing house. It was here that he **ran up against some opposition**. He seemed to **get off on the wrong foot**[5] with the publishers, who didn't like him and turned his book down. They're sorry now! A second publisher accepted his novel and it's already a best-seller world-wide.

[1] passed very easily (informal) [2] start doing something too quickly
[3] not very confident steps. You can also talk about *careful/tentative steps* when someone is doing something which they are not confident about.
[4] made great progress [5] make a bad start to a relationship

Exercises

50.1 **Choose the correct collocations in these holiday postcard messages.**

Hi Charlotte,
Fantastic weather here. We've been <u>making/going/getting</u> for long walks every day and usually <u>make/walk/take</u> a stroll along the beach every evening too. Even Bill <u>had/took/put</u> a few steps along the beach yesterday, and you know how lazy he is!
See you soon.
Gerry

Hi Josh,
Cambridge is a great place, the centre is small and everything is in walking distance. I'm really enjoying being able to go everywhere <u>on foot/on feet/by feet</u>. There are lovely parks where you can <u>make/run/go</u> jogging or just take a <u>brusque/brisk/ brush</u> walk. I usually <u>take/go for/make</u> a run every morning before breakfast. Will call you soon.
Love,
Meg

Hello Mum,
I'm having a great time here, but Chris hates it and spends all day <u>stepping /pacing/going</u> up and down in the hotel room wishing he was home! I usually just leave him and <u>make/do /go</u> running in the local park!
Love,
Steve

50.2 **Read the sentences in the box, then say if the statements below are true or false. If false, say why.**

> Polly strode confidently into the boss's office and asked for a pay rise.
> Mick just wandered aimlessly round the shops.
> Jade picked her way cautiously across the muddy field.
> Harry walked briskly towards the exit.
> Karen took a leisurely stroll through the park.

1 Jade moved quickly and cheerfully. TRUE / FALSE
2 Karen walked nervously and quite quickly. TRUE / FALSE
3 Polly walked quite quickly. TRUE / FALSE
4 Mick walked without any real purpose. TRUE / FALSE
5 Harry walked fairly slowly. TRUE / FALSE

50.3 **Complete B's responses using the words in brackets to make suitable collocations.**

1 A: Is everything going OK?
B: No, I'm afraid we've .... some problems. (RUN)
2 A: Is David making progress with his maths?
B: Yes, he's making .... (STRIDE)
3 A: Did Ed pass his exam?
B: Yes, he simply .... (WALK)
4 A: What sorts of people play golf? Is it just rich people?
B: No, not at all. There are people from all .... (WALK)
5 A: So James is not taking up Mark's offer of starting a business together?
B: Well, he said he needs time to think. He doesn't want to .... into it. (HEADLONG)
6 A: Is the town centre far from here?
B: No, it's only ten minutes. It's .... (WALK)

50.4 **Look up the word *run* in your dictionary. Make a note of three or four collocations.**

51 Starting and finishing

A Starting

PROMISING START FOR AMBROSE

Sally Ambrose, Britain's best hope in this year's Eurotennis tournament, **made a promising start** when she won her first match today against Sweden's Ulla Hemvik.

EARLY START TO HOLIDAY

Many people have decided to **make an early start** to the bank holiday weekend. Traffic was already building up on major motorways on Thursday evening.

ABSOLUTE BEGINNERS MAKE BEST LANGUAGE LEARNERS

Research shows that **absolute beginners** have a better chance of learning a language well than those who start with some knowledge.

ARTS FESTIVAL GETS OFF TO A GOOD START

The Glasgow Arts Festival **got off to a good start** this week, attracting more than 120,000 visitors during its first three days.

B Finishing

CLOSE FINISH IN SPANISH RALLY

Pedro Macarro emerged the winner of today's Spanish Grand Prix in a very **close finish**. Macarro was just 0.5 seconds ahead of Finland's Pekka Hirvonen.

TREATY BRINGS CIVIL WAR TO AN END

The 12-year civil war in Collocania was finally **brought to an end** yesterday when the two sides signed a peace treaty.

NEW CONSTITUTION

Ministers met today to **put the finishing touches** to a new constitution for the European Union.

ROUX JUST WINS

Claude Roux won the championship yesterday in a **nail-biting finish**.

C More collocations for starting and finishing

The invention of television **marked the beginning of the end** for popular radio shows.
I studied hard for a whole month and the **end result** was that I got a grade 'A' in the exam.
The meal we had on our last evening in Istanbul was a **perfect end** to our holiday.
It's two o'clock. Let's **make a start / get started**, shall we? Then we can finish by five.
As my time at university **came to an end**, I knew I had to start looking for a job.
The meeting **drew to a close** at 5.30, after a long discussion.
Without any warning, he was fired from the newspaper in 2004. It was an **abrupt end** to his career in journalism.

ERROR WARNING

We say that a holiday/journey/trip/meal **ended**, NOT ~~finished~~.

Exercises

51.1 What are the opposites of the underlined phrases in these sentences?

1 We can make a late start tomorrow if you like.
2 The competition has got off to a disappointing start as far as the British are concerned.
3 Meeting Josh on the beach on the last day was a horrible end to my holiday!
4 The meeting came to an unsatisfactory close.

51.2 Correct the collocation errors in these sentences.

1 It was such a near finish that no one was quite sure who had won.
2 I've just got to put the ending touches to my painting and then you can see it.
3 I expect the meeting will go to an end at about 5.30.
4 Everyone is here, so I think we should do a start now.
5 We all hope that the negotiations will succeed in taking the strike to an end.
6 E-mail marked the start of the end for the fax machine.
7 Our journey finished – as it had begun – in Cairo.
8 Have you heard yet what the finish result of the talks was?

51.3 Put the words in order to make sentences.

1 meeting / I / will soon / close / a / hope / draw / the / to
2 Town Hall / excellent reception / The conference / good / got / with / in / off / a / start / to / an / the
3 didn't / As / know / a single word / beginners' / Dan / was put / class / he / Japanese / absolute / an / of / in
4 as a politician / The / end / scandal / Jackson's / brought / abrupt / to / career/ an
5 won / nail-biting / a / Lance Armstrong / finish / cycle / the / race / in

51.4 Match the questions on the left with the responses on the right.

1 Do you think we should get started soon?
2 Did you already know some French when you started your course?
3 Was the race exciting?
4 Were you sad when your school days came to an end?
5 Did you enjoy the opera last night?
6 Do you know why their relationship came to such an abrupt end?

a No, it's a complete mystery to me.
b No, I was looking forward to university.
c Yes, most people are here now.
d No, I was an absolute beginner.
e Yes, the finish was nail-biting!
f Yes, it made the perfect end to a lovely day.

FOLLOW UP

Look up the words *begin*, *start*, *end* and *finish* in a good learner's dictionary and note down any other interesting collocations that you find there.

52 Talking about success and failure

A Success

Notice the collocations for talking about success in this schoolboy's end-of-term report.

SCHOOL REPORT

James Turner

MATHS:	James has **made a breakthrough** in his maths this year, doing excellent work in comparison with last year. A **remarkable achievement**.
ENGLISH:	This year has seen a **dramatic improvement** in James's English. His **crowning achievement** was his performance in the school production of Othello.
FRENCH:	James **has an excellent grasp of** French. This will **come in useful** for the school trip to France next year, and we hope he will **take advantage of** the opportunities to speak French there.
SCIENCE:	James has done very well this year, **passing his exams** without any problems. If he continues to work hard, his **success** next year **is guaranteed**.
GEOGRAPHY:	James has **made good progress** with his geography this year, **gaining good marks** in the end-of-year exam.
HISTORY:	James's history project was a **great success**. His use of original sources was **highly effective**. He **makes useful contributions** in class and **has the ability to** explain difficult ideas clearly to less able pupils.
ART:	James found some **effective ways** of working with natural materials this year and his self-portrait was a **brilliant success**.
SPORT:	James has been training hard and, as a member of the First Football Team, is now able to **enjoy the fruits of his hard work**. Playing for the school has certainly **brought out the best** in him and he has rightly **won the respect** of all his team-mates.

B Failure

Notice the collocations relating to failure in these extracts from a newspaper called *Today's Bad News*.

Unfortunately the peace talks now seem likely to **fail miserably**. [be totally unsuccessful]
Although a lot of money was invested in the film it has proved to be a **spectacular failure**. [extremely unsuccessful]
O'Connor's first play was a great success but his second **play flopped**. [failed to attract audiences]
Hopes that the play would enjoy a long run in London **were dashed**. [hopes have had to be abandoned]
Unfortunately, more pupils than ever are said to be **failing** their final **exams**.
The mountaineer's attempt to climb Mt Everest **went badly wrong**.
Everyone agrees that the peace talks are **doomed to failure**. [are certain to fail]
Hopes were initially high for the new project but it has proved to be a **dismal failure**. [a total failure]
A couple of major companies in the area **went out of business** last month. [stopped doing business]
I think the new plans for cutting railway costs **are a recipe for disaster**. [will certainly lead to major problems]
At the last moment the Olympic ski jumper **lost his nerve** and did not take part in the competition. [was not brave enough]
The President's speech was disappointing as it totally **missed the point**. [failed to understand what is really important]

Exercises

52.1 Look at A. Complete these speeches congratulating people on various types of success.

Over the years, Henry has (1) .... the respect of his colleagues, and now, as he retires, we all hope he can enjoy the (2) .... of his many years of hard work. His career has been a (3) .... success, and he has (4) .... an enormous contribution to our profession. Thank you from all of us.

As Head Teacher I am proud to say the school has had a great year. 87% of students (5) .... their exams with grades B or higher, while the remaining 13% (6) .... good or very good marks. The school rugby team has done well; its (7) .... achievement was winning the regional championship for the third year running. We believe that Garfham School (8) .... out the best in our boys and girls, and this year is no exception. Well done everyone!

Our research team has (9) .... a breakthrough this year, and I think we can say the success of the project is now (10) .... It has been a (11) .... achievement. We must now (12) .... advantage of the excellent progress we have (13) .... and find more (14) .... ways of persuading the public of the importance of our work. I know we (15) .... the ability to do this successfully, but we shall need all your support in this.

I am delighted to present our annual school Language prize to Tom Linton. Tom now has an excellent (16) .... of five major languages, which will certainly (17) .... in useful as he plans to work abroad. Tom was not always a brilliant language learner, but his work showed a (18) .... improvement last year, and his success has continued. Well done, Tom.

52.2 Match the beginning of each sentence on the left with its ending on the right.

1 Our plans went	miserably.
2 My hopes were	to failure.
3 After the horse threw me I lost	complete flop.
4 The scheme is doomed	disaster.
5 He failed his	business.
6 Our political campaign failed	point completely.
7 His plans are a recipe for	badly wrong.
8 A year later he went out of	dashed when I heard the news.
9 She seemed to miss the	final exams.
10 His latest novel was a	my nerve and couldn't get back on.

52.3 Correct the six collocation errors in this text.

I was always a dismal fail at school. I completely passed the point of maths and I failed sadly at most other subjects. Only the drama teacher managed to bring off the best in me and gave me a part in the school play. However, I lost my courage on the day of the performance and my hopes of a career on the stage were smashed.

53 Talking about cause and effect

A Different 'cause' verbs

topic	*verb*	*examples*
negative events, situations and feelings	cause	The storm **caused chaos** / **havoc** / **a lot of damage**. Her remarks **caused alarm/concern**. Her son's behaviour **caused her great anxiety** / **a lot of embarrassment**.
positive and negative changes	bring about	The discovery of X-rays **brought about a revolution/ transformation** in medical science. The events **brought about the downfall/collapse** of the government.
positive and negative situations and feelings	create	His book helped **create awareness** of inner-city poverty. Your presence on the committee is **creating problems** for all of us.
sudden, often negative, events	spark off	The announcement **sparked off riots/demonstrations** in the cities. His wife's absence **sparked off rumours** in the media.
reactions from people	attract	His book has **attracted** a lot of **criticism/interest**. The charity appeal **attracted support** from a wide range of people.
results and effects	produce	My comments **produced the opposite effect** to what I intended. His research has not yet **produced any results**, but we must wait.

B Causes and effects

The **immediate cause** of the problem was an oil leak.	The **underlying cause** of the problem was a lack of funds over many years.
The government hopes to **reduce/minimise the impact** of the new taxes.	The support she got from the Prime Minister **strengthened/increased the impact** of her report.
The new measures had an **unexpected/ unforeseen outcome**.	The new tax led to the **predictable/inevitable outcome** that many people became poorer.
The **positive/beneficial effects** of the changes were soon apparent.	The **negative/adverse effects** of the changes were not noticed immediately.
The crisis was the **direct/inevitable result** of bad economic planning.	One **indirect/unforeseen result** of the new laws has been a rise in unemployment.

C Common expressions for everyday events

The book **caused an uproar** in the United States. [made a lot of people complain angrily]
If you make him angry, you'll have to **suffer the consequences**.
The accident **had a huge effect** on her life.
Latino singers have **had a major impact** on pop music this year.
Remember that it **makes/creates a bad impression** if you're late.
The drug companies **have a lot of influence** on doctors.
Their love affair **caused a sensation**.

ERROR WARNING

To *affect* means 'to have an influence on someone/something, or to cause them to change'. (Her death **affected** everyone **deeply**.) To *effect* means 'to achieve something / make something happen'. (We are trying to **effect a change** in the way people think about their diet.) The noun *effect(s)* refers to the result(s) of something. (His stressful life **has had an effect** on his health.)

Exercises

53.1 Complete each sentence with a verb from A. Use each verb once only.

1 The film has .... a lot of criticism, both positive and negative.
2 The extra work Olga's had to do has .... her a lot of stress.
3 The experiment didn't .... the results we'd expected.
4 David Line wrote an excellent article on the factors that .... the collapse of the Soviet Union.
5 The rise in the price of fuel has .... a series of protests.

53.2 Choose the correct collocation.

I've just been reading the very interesting biography of Rhoda Legge, an early star of silent films. She isn't generally well-known now but she caused a(n) (1) *impression / sensation / outcome* in the 1920s when she had an affair with a minor member of a European royal family. This turned out to have a (2) *major / principal / chief* impact on her career. At first she was very distressed by the (3) *effect / influence / uproar* it caused in the press. However, ultimately, she did not suffer the negative (4) *results / consequences / outcomes* she initially feared. On the contrary, the affair had an (5) *unpredicted / unknown / unexpected* outcome. The (6) *good / advantageous / positive* effects of the affair soon began to make themselves felt as she began to be offered all sorts of interesting new roles. The affair (7) *affected / effected / infected* the way people thought about her. The relationship did not last more than a few months but it (8) *produced / attracted / caused* a sensation that (9) *had / did / got* a huge impact on her movie career.

53.3 Choose an ending from the box to complete each sentence below.

some changes in the way the college is structured.
the development of personality very deeply.
the impact of the tragedy on our children.
result of the huge tax rises.
a considerable influence on his choice of career.
cause of the fire was.
the impact of the new measures.
results which no one could have predicted.
a good impression at a job interview.
causes of crime.

1 The enquiry aims to establish what the immediate
2 Henry's grandmother had
3 The changes had some unforeseen
4 Criticising your previous boss doesn't create
5 We must do all we can to minimise
6 What happens in childhood affects
7 Management is trying to effect
8 The TV coverage they have received has strengthened
9 The government should do something about the underlying
10 The riots were an inevitable

FOLLOW UP

Look up the words *influence*, *effect*, *impact* and *consequence* in a good learner's dictionary. Make a note of any other interesting collocations that you find.

54 Remembering and sensing

A Remembering

Notice all the memory collocations in this dialogue between two old school friends.

Beth: I saw Terry last night. Do you remember her? We were at school together.

Tom: No, my **long-term memory**[1] is terrible these days. Come to think of it, my **short-term memory**[2] isn't that brilliant either. And I used to **have** such **a good memory**! Anyway, **give me a clue**[3].

Beth: She was the one with long black hair and glasses. You always used to say that she **reminded** you **strongly** of that singer you used to like.

Tom: Oh, yes. I **vaguely remember** her now. She used to be friends with Jo, didn't she?

Beth: Yes. I'd **clean forgotten**[4] about her too. She ran over to me in the street and said hello. My **mind went blank**[5]. I could **remember her face** but I'd **completely forgotten her name**. But once we started talking, the **memories came flooding back**[6]. My **earliest memory** of her is that we all went to the beach with her parents one weekend when we were about 12.

Tom: Oh yes. Now you're **stirring up memories**[7] for me. I can **distinctly remember** being stung by a jellyfish in the water.

Beth: I can see why you wanted to **blot out that memory**[8]!

Tom: I can **vividly remember** it now though. Actually, the whole weekend was an **unforgettable experience**. We told ghost stories all night **if I remember rightly**.

Beth: Oh yes, that's right. Now I **remember it well**. It's terrible how **memories fade**[9] as time passes, isn't it! Mind you, I'm happy to lose some of my more **painful memories** of school.

[1] memory of what happened a long time ago
[2] memory of what happened recently
[3] informal: tell me something more to help me
[4] informal: completely forgotten
[5] I couldn't remember anything
[6] lots of memories returned
[7] making old memories come back
[8] avoid remembering something unpleasant
[9] memories get less clear

> **ERROR WARNING** *I've forgotten my homework I left it at home.* NOT I've forgotten my homework at home.

B Sensing

Read these problem letters from a magazine and notice the collocations relating to sensing.

When I first met my new boss, I **had/got the impression** that he might be a difficult person to work for. I **sensed** some **tension** between us. Now I **have a feeling** that he is trying to make things difficult for me. I don't know whether I should **trust my intuition**[1] and hand in my resignation. Or am I just being **ridiculously over-sensitive**?

For the last few weeks I've been much more **sensitive to heat** and **sensitive to light** than I used to be. I've always had **sensitive skin** and **sensitive teeth** but this is much worse than ever before. My hands have also started **going numb**[2] if I get at all cold. I used to have an **acute**[3] **sense of smell** and **acute hearing** but I don't any more.

[1] feel confident that my instinctive feelings are correct
[2] losing all feeling
[3] acute = sharp, very good

> **ERROR WARNING** Remember the difference between a **sensitive person** [a person who is easily upset] and a **sensible person** [a person with good judgement].

Exercises

54.1 **These people are all talking about their memories of childhood. Use words from A opposite to complete the collocations. The words in brackets give the meaning of the word you need.**

1

Well, my .... (*first*) memory is of sitting in our garden on my mother's lap. I .... (*not very clearly*) remember that there was a cat or dog there too, but I can't remember much else.

2

I used to have a .... memory when I was young, but I'm 82 now, and as you get older your .... memory (*memory for things that happened long ago*) is very clear, but your .... memory (*memory for things that happened recently*) is less good. Sometimes I can't remember what happened yesterday. But I can .... (*very clearly*) remember my first day at school as a child.

3

My mother sometimes tells me things I did or said when I was little but which I've .... (*totally*) forgotten. One embarrassing memory which I'd rather .... out (*avoid remembering*) is when I took some scissors and cut my own hair. It looked awful!

4

Seeing schoolchildren often .... up all kinds of memories (*makes old memories come to the surface*) for me. I wasn't happy at school and I have some .... (*unpleasant*) memories of being forced to do sports, which I hated. Sometimes, when I hear certain songs, memories come .... back (*lots of memories return*).

54.2 **Complete the collocations connected with remembering.**

1 It was a nightmare. The moment I looked at the exam paper my mind went ....
2 Her name's Lyn, and she worked with Nick a few years ago, if I remember ....
3 Let me see if I can remember where we met. Give me a ....
4 It was a wonderful trip to India. It was a(n) .... experience.

54.3 **Complete each sentence using a word from the box.**

intuition	sensitive	numb	acute	impression	sensible	over-sensitive	sensed

1 Do you ever get the .... that Jane is a little mad? She says some very odd things.
2 I .... a bit of tension between Mark and Pauline. I wonder if they've had a row?
3 Usually I can trust my .... to tell me if someone is lying or not.
4 You're ridiculously ....! You treat everything I say as a personal attack on you.
5 It was so cold and I had no gloves on. My hands went .... as I rode my bike.
6 He uses a special face cream and toothpaste as he has .... skin and teeth.
7 Dogs have .... hearing and smell, and are often used to rescue disaster victims.
8 Paul is a very .... person; you can trust him not to do anything foolish.

54.4 **Choose the correct collocation.**

1 I *distinctly / strongly / rightly* remember that we agreed to meet at the gym.
2 I *made / had / took* the impression that you didn't like Molly.
3 You must wear gloves in this cold or your fingers will *do / have / go* numb.
4 I usually find that I can *trust / rely / depend* my intuition.
5 I'd rather *stir up / flood back / blot out* such unpleasant memories.

55 Agreeing and disagreeing

A Verb and noun collocations

collocation	*example*
go along with an idea / a view	I **go along with your view** that crime and poverty are linked.
be in (complete) agreement	We **are in complete agreement** over the question of drug abuse in athletics.
tend to agree/disagree	I **tend to agree** that parents often blame teachers for problems which start within the family.
share an opinion / a view	I **share your opinion** that sport is over-commercialised.
appreciate someone's point of view	I **appreciate your point of view**, but I still think you are overstating the problem.
see someone's point [understand their opinion]	I can **see your point**; I've never thought of it in that way before.
enter into an argument	I'd prefer not to **enter into an argument** over the war in Collocania.
differences arise/exist	**Differences exist / have arisen** between the unions and the management over how to solve the problem.
come to / reach a compromise	We disagree over what to do, but I'm sure we can **come to / reach a compromise.**
settle a dispute / your differences	The management and the union have finally **settled their pay dispute**. I'm sure we can **settle our differences** without damaging our friendship.
agree to differ [agree to have different opinions]	I don't think we will ever agree with each other. We'll just have to **agree to differ**.

B Verb and adverb collocations

verb	*adverb*	*example*
agree	entirely/ wholeheartedly	I **entirely agree** with you on the question of nuclear waste.
agree	partly/up to a point	I **agree up to a point**, but I also think there are other important factors.
disagree	fundamentally/ totally/strongly	The two philosophers **disagreed fundamentally** over the effect of the environment on behaviour.

C Adjective and noun collocations for disputes and strong disagreements

I've often disagreed strongly with Nancy but I've never had such a **head-on clash** with her before. [disagreement where two people confront each other directly]
The **bitter dispute** between the two groups finally led to violence.
We had a very **heated argument** about immigration the other day.
Jeff and I had a **fundamental disagreement** over who should be the next Chair of the club.

D Further collocations for agreeing and disagreeing

The Regional Education Committee has reached a **unanimous agreement** on a new system of exams for secondary schools.
Controversy continues to **exist/rage** over the appointment of the new Director.
A **conflict of opinion** within the National Olympic Association is threatening to delay the building of a new stadium.

Exercises

55.1 **Look at A. Make collocations by matching words from the circle on the left with words from the oval on the right.**

agree
enter
appreciate
be
share
come
settle
see

to differ
in agreement
an opinion
others' points of view
into an argument
to a compromise
our differences
someone's point

55.2 **Put the expressions from the box into the appropriate category below.**

a controversy rages a head-on clash a heated argument
settle a dispute come to a compromise differences exist

reaching agreement	*disagreeing*

55.3 **Rewrite each sentence using the word in brackets, so that it keeps the same meaning.**

1 I don't completely agree with what you say. (POINT)
2 I am in total agreement with you. (ENTIRELY)
3 There was no disagreement among the committee members. (UNANIMOUS)
4 There will always be differences of opinion even between friends. (ARISE)
5 James and Brian had a big disagreement over the question of climate change. (STRONGLY)
6 The project has been delayed because of the different opinions among the members of the committee. (CONFLICT)
7 I find it difficult to agree with such an idea. (ALONG)
8 We are in total disagreement about most things. (FUNDAMENTALLY)

55.4 **Answer these questions about the collocations on the opposite page.**

1 Which collocation suggests that a disagreement is like a high temperature?
2 Which two collocations suggest that a disagreement is like a fight or a war?
3 Which collocation suggests that controversy is like anger?
4 Why do you think the word *bitter* is used to refer to quarrels and disputes as well as to taste?
5 Which collocation suggests that understanding someone's opinion is like using your eyes?

56 Talking about beliefs and opinions

A Speaking about beliefs and opinions

[1] what many people think

[2] are completely different

[3] disagreement

[4] I'm beginning to think

B More formal ways of discussing beliefs

Look at this extract from a student essay and notice the collocations referring to beliefs.

The writer seems to **make assumptions**[1] based on an **unshakeable belief** in the superiority of his own value system. He seems to be unaware of the extent to which his own **set of beliefs** has **coloured his judgement**[2]. His research **leads him to conclude** that military action was justified. However, his **evidence is based on** one single document and **attaches** too much **importance** to this. I do not **trust his judgement**. Moreover, other documents **cast doubt on**[3] his conclusions. **Opinions** on the issue **are divided**[4] and my own **considered opinion**[5] is that the writer is not to be trusted. I **have serious misgivings about**[6] his research and I **have doubts** about the accuracy of some of his facts.

[1] thinks or says things are true without enough evidence
[2] affected his judgement
[3] suggest something may be wrong with
[4] people have different opinions
[5] opinion after much thought
[6] I have serious doubts about

C Some error warnings

The expressions in this table are collocations that learners often have difficulty with.

collocation	*comment*
I **hope you'll come** to my party.	NOT ~~wish~~
They've **given up hope** of any survivors.	NOT ~~the~~ hope
We need to **think hard** about this problem.	NOT ~~consider~~ hard – could be **consider** this problem **carefully**
I wish they would just **leave me alone**.	NOT ~~let~~
Many people **hold the view/opinion** that …	NOT ~~meaning~~
He **has strong opinions** on many subjects.	NOT ~~heavy~~ or ~~big~~

Exercises

56.1 Look at A. Complete the collocations in these letters to a newspaper.

Sir/Madam,
I (1) .... the opinion of your correspondent that the EU has brought peace to Europe, but I cannot agree that a single currency for all of Europe is necessary. It is a (2) .... of opinion whether economic stability can be maintained with one currency, and there is (3) .... to believe that some European economies were more stable before they joined the euro.
Yours,
A. Tory

Sir/Madam,
According to popular (4) ...., the war between Gronbia and Karzkut started with a (5) .... of opinion over how best to preserve the beautiful mountain environment on both sides of the border between them. The two countries were apparently (6) .... apart on how to approach the issue, and war resulted. If this is indeed true, how stupid can human beings become?
Yours sincerely,
B. Leaver

Sir/Madam,
While I (7) .... believe in the right of everyone to own a car, I am also a great (8) .... in keeping fit and healthy. The government tells us we must take exercise, but I have a (9) .... suspicion that they are afraid of saying we should sell our cars because they would lose billions in road taxes.
Yours,
A. Sighklist

56.2 Correct the seven collocation errors in this text.

I wish we can solve a big problem we have regarding our student committee. Opinions are separated about how to approach the issue and, naturally, some members have very heavy opinions. Some of their views are based on their unstirred belief that they are always right and that no one can challenge their group of beliefs. My own thoughtful opinion is that we should have new elections, but I know that others have quite a different meaning.

56.3 Match each verb in the box with its noun collocation in the table below. Then write one sentence for each collocation.

cast colour attach make have trust

	verb	*noun*
1		assumptions
2		somebody's judgement
3		
4		importance to
5		doubt on
6		serious misgivings doubts

56.4 Make seven collocations using the words in the box. Use each word once only.

apart belief believe cast think firmly hard opinions
sneaking strong suspicion doubt poles popular

57 Deciding and choosing

A Decisions and judgements

Note the collocations in bold in these e-mails between colleagues.

Hi Rita,
Have you **made a decision** yet about the new job? It must be difficult. It's such a **big decision** to have to move to London and everything. I always **put off making decisions** till the last possible moment. I bet you're the same. I detected a **slight hesitation** in your last e-mail. Are you **having second thoughts**? Anyway, let me know.
Paul

Dear Carl,
You've probably heard that the management have **taken the decision** to close the Madrid office. There was a lot of discussion, but apparently it was a **unanimous decision** in the end. There's always been a **degree of uncertainty** surrounding the future of the Madrid office, but let's just hope this will now be seen as a **wise decision** by everyone.
Jane

Dear Mary,
After weeks of hesitating, it seems Archie has **arrived at a decision** about the research fund. He's going to increase it by £10,000. I think that's a **sensible decision** that combines generosity and **sound judgement**. But he's also **defending his decision** to close down the San Antonio project, which is losing a lot of money. However, he's **reserving judgement** on the Berlin project until he gets more reliable information.
Nick

B Choices, opportunities, advice

Tim: I'm going to have to **make a choice** soon about next year. I've been **given the chance** of going on a six-month expedition to South America and I've been offered a job in a bookshop here.

Laura: Wow! South America! That sounds like **the opportunity of a lifetime**! How could you say no?

Tim: Well, believe it or not, I don't have **a burning desire** to see the world, I'd **much prefer** just to stay at home. Anyway, I'm going to **consider** all **the options** before I decide.

Laura: Well, I know you never **take** my **advice** but I would **strongly advise** you to think of the future. Overseas experience is much more useful than working in your home town. You're lucky to **have a choice**, a lot of people stay at home because they **have no option**.

Tim: I know, I know, but it's a **tough choice**. You wouldn't understand.

Laura: Well I think you're just **taking** the **soft option** if you choose the bookshop. I can't believe you're going to **pass up the opportunity** of a trip to South America.

Tim: Well, we all **face difficult choices** now and then.

Laura: Difficult! You're mad! Look, just don't **reject** South America **out of hand.** Promise me you'll think about it.

Tim: Yes, yes, I already said I'm going to **weigh up the options** and **come to a decision**.

TIP Horoscopes often focus on choices and decisions in people's lives. Read horoscopes in English and note any new collocations connected with decisions and choices.

Exercises

57.1 **Using collocations from section A on the opposite page, complete B's remarks in these conversations so that B agrees with what A says.**

1 A: I still don't know whether to take the job or not. But I'll have to decide soon.
B: Yes, you can't go on putting .... the decision for ever.
2 A: It was good that absolutely everyone agreed in the end, wasn't it?
B: Yes, I'm glad it was a .... decision.
3 A: I think I'd prefer to wait and see what happens before judging the new system.
B: Yes, I think it's best if we all .... judgement till we see the results.
4 A: I said I would join the committee but now I'm not so sure.
B: Mm, it's obvious you're having .... thoughts.
5 A: I felt he was hesitating a little bit before deciding, didn't you?
B: Yes, I definitely detected a .... hesitation on his part, you're right.

57.2 **Complete each sentence using a word from the box.**

degree	come	wise	take	sound	defend	give	tough	arrive	weigh

1 She has always been respected for her .... judgement in financial matters.
2 Do you think it was a .... decision to sell off the company's Dublin branch? I think it was a mistake.
3 I think we should .... up the options before deciding.
4 It took the committee a whole day to .... at a decision.
5 There seems to be a .... of uncertainty as to whether they will sign the contract.
6 I don't think we can .... our decision to exclude some of the children from the competition. Everyone thinks it's very unfair.
7 It was a .... choice, but we had to make it, even though we hated doing so.
8 I think you should .... your father's advice and say no.
9 I wish someone would .... me the chance to prove how good I am.
10 Have you .... to a decision yet about your university course?

57.3 **Read these remarks by different people, then answer the questions.**

Rhoda: I think I'll choose the supermarket job; the job at the children's hospital seems like very hard work. I want something easy.
Zubaya: I've decided to say no to the offer to join the conservation team in Canada.
Kim: I desperately want to see the world; I'll take any job if it means I can travel.
Archie: I don't want to sell my flat but I have no other way of getting money.
Mabel: Me, work in a zoo? Never, absolutely not! I'm not even prepared to consider it!
Elaine: I've been offered a job singing on a cruise ship. It's fantastic! I'll never get an offer like this, ever again.

	name
1 Who is going to do something because they have no option?	
2 Who has been given the opportunity of a lifetime?	
3 Who wants to take the soft option?	
4 Who is rejecting something out of hand?	
5 Who has decided to pass up an opportunity?	
6 Who has a burning desire to do something?	

58 Claiming and denying

A Making accusations

A government minister is today **facing accusations** of taking bribes. There have been **heavy hints**[1] about this for some time. An article in *The Moon* last week **clearly implied**[2] that a top political figure was involved in a scandal and **dropped** a number of **broad hints**[3] as to who it was. A **leaked document**[4] published in today's *Moon*, however, **makes** a number of **serious allegations**[5], which **openly accuse** the Minister of corruption. The Minister has **issued a statement**[6], saying **the claims are unfounded**[7]. He claims that he has been **wrongly accused** by *The Moon* because of its **long-running battle**[8] with the government.

1 strong suggestions
2 suggested clearly but indirectly
3 made a number of obvious suggestions
4 an official document unofficially given to the press
5 makes serious claims of criminal behaviour
6 made a formal statement
7 the claims are untrue, have no basis in reality
8 an argument that has been going on for a long time

B Putting forward a point of view

Jones **puts forward** an interesting **theory**[1] of language learning, **backing up**[2] his **argument** with thorough data. **Fully accepting** the fact that different learners find different methods useful, Jones **makes the point**[3] that motivation is the key factor in most learners' success. Although this has been **widely acknowledged**[4] in general terms for some time, Jones is more precise than most, **stating clearly** that motivation is more important than all other factors, and **substantiating**[5] this **claim** with impressive data.

1 proposes a theory 2 supporting 3 presents an argument
4 accepted by many people 5 supporting

C Denying

collocation	*example*
strongly deny	The PM **strongly denied** claims of corruption made against him.
deny charges / an accusation	Despite the evidence against him, the accused **denied the charges**.
deny a rumour / an allegation	The pop star has **denied all the rumours** about her marriage.
disclaim responsibility	The hotel **disclaims all responsibility** for guests' vehicles.
reject an idea / a suggestion	Ann **rejected** all Joe's **suggestions** about how to decorate their flat.
run contrary to	The research findings **run contrary to** popular belief.
contradictory evidence/advice	**Contradictory evidence** made it hard for the jury to reach a verdict.

ERROR WARNING

Note these collocations: **deny/reject a claim**, **deny a rumour / an allegation / an accusation** but **reject an idea / a suggestion** and **refuse an invitation/offer**. You **deny/reject/refuse something**. You **deny that something** is true. You can also **refuse to do something** (in the future) but **deny doing something** (in the past).

Exercises

58.1 Complete the sentences, using collocations from A.

1 A .... provided the press with information about the government's secret plans.
2 Management has been having a .... with trade union representatives over a number of aspects of employees' rights.
3 I'm going to get my son an iPod for his birthday. He's been dropping .... about what he wants for some time.
4 At the end of the three-day meeting a spokesperson will .... to inform the press about any agreements that have been signed.
5 A front-page article in today's paper is making some .... about the behaviour of some top international bankers.
6 The article did not name anyone directly but it .... who was involved.

58.2 Fill each gap in this extract from a scientific article.

In his latest article on the free market Milton King puts (1) .... some original theories. He (2) .... earlier ideas which up until now most economists have accepted without question. He (3) .... some fascinating points based on his own extensive research which is widely (4) .... as an important contribution to economic thought. The data from his research (5) .... up his theories and help to (6) .... his claim that modern economies would benefit from major reforms.

58.3 Replace the underlined words with an appropriate form of either *deny*, *reject* or *refuse* to give the sentences the opposite meaning.

1 The politician <u>agreed</u> that the allegations made against him were true.
2 I think we should <u>accept</u> Jill's invitation to their New Year's Party, don't you?
3 Hill <u>accepts</u> the theories put forward by Jackson.
4 Katie <u>agreed</u> that she had been present at the meeting.
5 I hope they will <u>accept</u> my offer of help.

58.4 Rewrite each sentence using the word in brackets, so that it keeps the same meaning.

1 We are not responsible for valuables that are not left in the hotel safe. (DISCLAIM)
2 The pop star insisted that there was no basis to the claims made against him. (UNFOUNDED)
3 Jones's views do not accord with the facts. (RUN)
4 The newspaper clearly suggested who the actor's new lover was. (DROPPED)
5 Paul insisted that what people were saying about him was untrue. (DENIED)
6 Whatever idea I suggest, Jim says it is no good. (REJECTS)
7 I don't know what to do, as everyone keeps suggesting I do something different. (CONTRADICTORY)
8 The student is being accused of cheating in his exam. (FACING)
9 In his new book the writer presents an interesting theory of art. (FORWARD)
10 Recent research supports McIntyre's theory. (UP)

59 Liking and disliking

A Strong statements: nouns and adjectives

noun	*collocations*
liking	I **have a particular liking** for quiet, relaxing music. She **had a genuine liking** for her cousins.
love	His **great love** of nature can be seen in his paintings. Her **passionate love** of the sea inspired her to sail round the world.
regard [formal]	I have always had the **greatest regard** for her. She has the **highest regard** for her teacher.
enjoyment	I will never forget the **sheer enjoyment** of listening to the children singing. We get **great enjoyment** out of our little cottage in the mountains.
pleasure	It's been a **great pleasure** meeting you. I hope we meet again. It was such a **huge pleasure** to be able to relax and do nothing for a week.
preference	When asked, many people expressed a **clear preference** for organic food. I've always had a **strong preference** for short stories rather than novels.
dislike	I have an **intense dislike** of rock music that is played too loud. She **took an instant dislike to** Mr Peabody, but she did not know why.
aversion[1]	He has always had a **huge aversion** to hard work of any kind. Most people have a **strong aversion** to excessive violence on TV.
hatred	She had a **deep hatred** of politicians, especially corrupt ones. The **deep-rooted hatred** between the two tribes led to a bloody civil war.

[1] a feeling of strong dislike or a lack of willingness to do something

B Verbs and nouns

These people are talking about their favourite airlines.

I think Globe Air are pretty good. You can **state** your **preference** for a special low fat menu, or seafood or vegetarian. They have great in-flight entertainment too – they try to **cater for** everyone's **tastes**. They seem to **take pride in** their service.

I do a lot of long-distance flying and I **don't relish the thought**[1] of a twelve-hour flight with no leg-room, so I usually fly with Arrow. They give you a lot of space, even in economy. And they seem to **take pleasure** in looking after you.

[1] don't like to think that it is going to happen

I think most people **take offence**[2] if they're just treated like a number. I **have no sympathy** for airlines that lose customers because they're too lazy to **give** them **a warm welcome** when they step on board. Visa Airlines are always very friendly.

[2] become upset because someone has insulted or disrespected them

C Other useful collocations for likes and dislikes

I like most James Bond Films, but *Goldfinger* is my **absolute/all-time favourite.**
I've always been a **great lover** of Mozart's operas.
She's a(n) **ardent[1]/dedicated fan** of American football. [[1]showing strong feelings]
I'm a **keen admirer** of President Futral of Collocania. He is such a strong leader.
My wife's father always **filled me with admiration.** He achieved so much during his life.
It always **gives** me **pleasure** when I see my children doing well at school.

Exercises

59.1 **Look at A. Rewrite each sentence using the word in brackets, so that it keeps the same meaning.**

1 In the survey most people said they much preferred coffee to tea. (PREFERENCE)
2 Karl really dislikes people using mobile phones in restaurants. (AVERSION)
3 The staff all think very highly of their managing director. (REGARD)
4 I've enormously enjoyed getting to know you. (PLEASURE)
5 Suzie genuinely likes cowboy films. (GENUINE)
6 My parents absolutely detest most modern architecture. (HATRED)
7 We enormously enjoy our weekends in the country. (GREAT)
8 Rex knew at once that he could never like his new secretary. (INSTANT)

59.2 **Mark the statements with + if they are about liking and – if they are about disliking.**

1 I have no sympathy for anyone who takes such foolish risks.
2 Jane Austen is my all-time favourite writer.
3 I'm a dedicated fan of Robin Williams.
4 I don't relish the thought of a holiday with all my cousins.
5 It gives me no pleasure to have to say this to you.
6 I take pride in doing my work as neatly as I can.
7 I must say I rather took offence at what she said to me.
8 I'm a great lover of the open air life.
9 I've always been a keen admirer of Nelson Mandela.

59.3 **Choose the correct collocation.**

I went to a new Italian restaurant last night. It claimed to (1) *cater / cook / feed* for everyone's tastes. I went there with my brother. We both have a (2) *large / heavy / strong* preference for Italian food. We also both have a (3) *peculiar / special / particular* liking for sitting out-of-doors and this restaurant had a lovely garden. Unfortunately, the food did not (4) *make / give / pass* us quite so much pleasure. Although the staff gave us a very (5) *warm / hot / boiling* welcome when we arrived, they didn't seem to (6) *take / do / make* much pride in their service or their cooking. I certainly don't much relish the (7) *suggestion / proposal / thought* of going there again.

59.4 **Answer these questions.**

1 Does it give you more pleasure to give a present or to receive a present?
2 Are you more likely to take an intense dislike to a person or a place?
3 If you are asked to state your preference for a window or an aisle seat on a plane, what do you normally go for?
4 Which singer is your absolute favourite?
5 Name one person who has filled you with admiration in the last five years.
6 Do you take more pride in your work or your home?
7 Name three people or things that you feel great love for.
8 Do you get more pleasure from reading or from listening to music?

60 Praising and criticising

A Praising

Read this review of a theatre production from a local newspaper.

I have **nothing but praise for** this production of *Dogs* and **offer my congratulations** to all the cast. The **thunderous applause** at the end of **last night's performance** was **richly deserved**. The actors had managed to **put on a** simply **dazzling production**. James King, in particular, **gave an outstanding performance**. Of course, the cast cannot **take full credit for** its success; we must also **warmly congratulate** the producer. He has **received critical acclaim**[1] many times in the past. He **justly deserves** all the **rave reviews**[2] he will undoubtedly receive from many others as well as myself. We must also **give credit** to the production's wardrobe department. I am sure they will also **win** a lot of **praise** for their original and exciting costumes.

1 enthusiastic words
2 very enthusiastic review [informal]

Also note these collocations relating to praise:

The orchestra **received a standing ovation** for their performance of the symphony. [the audience liked the performance so much that they stood up to applaud]
Your boss **thinks the world of** you. He's always **singing your praises** to me. [informal]
My parents always used to **speak well/highly of** that journalist.
Her father **warmly/heartily approves** of her new boyfriend.
I hope you will **give your blessing** to the plan. [say you wish it well]
Let's **give** the winner **a big clap / a round of applause.**
You deserve **a pat on the back** for such excellent marks! [you deserve praise]

B Criticising

When you are criticised you **come in for criticism.** You may **respond to this criticism,** you may **counter the criticism** [criticise your critic back] or you may **dismiss the criticism** [say it is untrue or unimportant].
A person may **show his/her disapproval** or **express his/her disapproval** and this is often done by giving a **look of disapproval** or with a **frown of disapproval.**

word	*collocates with*	*example*
criticism	harsh [strong], constant, constructive [useful]	The play came in for some **harsh criticism**.
critical	highly and sharply	The writer is **sharply critical** of our political system.
criticise	roundly [thoroughly], fiercely, bitterly	He was **roundly criticised** for his rudeness.
a critic	harsh, outspoken [critic who says exactly what s/he thinks]	Actors fear him because he is such an **outspoken critic**.
disapprove of	strongly, thoroughly	I **strongly disapprove of** smoking.
condemn	severely	The politician was **severely condemned** for his dishonesty.
condemnation	wholesale, universal [both mean by (almost) everyone]	The country's aggressive behaviour has earned **universal condemnation**.
object to	strongly, strenuously [with a lot of effort]	Local residents **strenuously objected to** the development plans.

Exercises

60.1 **Complete these extracts from TV programmes where the speakers are praising people.**

For this young violinist, Nuria Shilov, her performance ends with a (1).................... ovation and (2).................... applause. Her playing has received critical (3).................... in the last year in her home country, and now her talent has been recognised by an international audience.

Now the President of the National Badminton Federation (4).................... congratulates Wang Shih-Ping on his (5).................... deserved victory in this year's tournament. His skilful playing has (6).................... a lot of praise from commentators, though he personally refuses to (7).................... full credit for his achievements, and (8).................... credit instead to his manager, Karla Ennaise.

Well, the team manager is ecstatic and is at this moment making a speech (9).................... the praises of the captain, Blake Samson, and the rest of the team. And there is no doubt that they (10).................... deserve all this praise for such a remarkable victory.

So, at the end of this week's quiz, the blue team have won. Let me (11).................... my congratulations to you all. You'll be coming back next week. And let's give the losers a (12).................... of applause. The red team also played a great game.

60.2 **Circle T (True) or F (False) after each statement. If you circle F, say why.**

1 If you speak highly of someone, you praise them. T F
2 If you have nothing but praise for someone, you do not approve of what they do. T F
3 If you criticise someone roundly, you criticise them only slightly. T F
4 If you heartily approve of something, you are in favour of it. T F
5 If you counter criticism, you just accept it. T F
6 If someone gives their blessing to something, they are against it. T F
7 If you give someone a clap, it is usually because you like what they have done. T F
8 If you give constructive criticism, you normally have a positive intention. T F

60.3 **Put the words in order to make sentences.**

1 lot / He / in / for / criticism / a / of / came
2 criticism / the / responded / of / to / disapprove / how / I / thoroughly / she
3 him / condemned / lying / for / severely / judge / The
4 disapproval / my / behaviour / of / want / I / express / to / her
5 outspoken / were / but / dismissed / critics / he / The / criticisms / their
6 comments / condemnation / His / universal / received
7 objected / plan / We / and / strenuously / the / to / were / critical / it / highly / of
8 always / a / government / been / I /critic / of / have / corrupt / harsh

60.4 **Complete the collocations in this text.**

This is the last exercise in this book. May we give you a pat on the .... for getting to this point. Indeed, you .... deserve a .... clap. We have .... but praise for you and would like to .... you our warm congratulations!

Key

Unit 1

1.1 1 A collocation is a pair or group of words which are often used together in a way which sounds natural to native speakers of English.
2 *car* and *food*
3 *narrow-minded, teapot* and *car park*
4 idioms

1.2 make mistakes
powerful engine
have breakfast
make an effort
watch TV
ancient monument
substantial meal
bitterly cold
pitch dark
strictly forbidden
Other possible collocations are: make breakfast, substantial breakfast.

1.3 The first four statements are all true. The final statement is probably not true. You may well be understood if you use less natural collocations but you will not sound as you probably wish to sound.

1.4

compound	*collocation*	*idiom*
teapot	make a mistake	pull somebody's leg
key ring	heavy snow	a storm in a tea cup
checkpoint	valid passport	
	bitterly disappointed	
	live music	

1.5 The most useful collocations to learn are underlined here.

When I left university I made a decision to take up a profession in which I could be creative. I could play the guitar, but I'd never written any songs. Nonetheless I decided to become a singer-songwriter. I made some recordings but I had a rather heavy cold so they didn't sound good. I made some more, and sent them to a record company and waited for them to reply. So, while I was waiting to become famous, I got a job in a fast-food restaurant. That was five years ago. I'm still doing the same job.

Unit 2

2.1 All of the underlined phrases are strong collocations.

My friend Beth is desperately worried about her son at the moment. He wants to enrol on a course of some sort but just can't make a decision about what to study. I gave Beth a ring and we had a long chat about it last night. She said he'd like to study for a degree but is afraid he won't meet the requirements for university entry. Beth thinks he should do a course in Management because he'd like to set up his own business in the future. I agreed that that would be a wise choice.

2.2 1 She's having a party.
2 She's taking an exam.
3 She's giving a lecture. / She's giving a party.
4 She's making good progress.
5 She's doing her duty. / [informal] She's doing an exam.

2.3 In the morning I ~~made~~ **did** some work in the garden then I ~~spent~~ **had** a rest for about an hour before going out to ~~have~~ **do** some shopping in town. It was my sister's birthday and I wanted to ~~do~~ **make** a special effort to cook a nice meal for her. I ~~gave~~ **had** (or **took**) a look at a new Thai cookery book in the bookshop and decided to buy it. It has some ~~totally~~ **very/quite/extremely** easy recipes and I managed to ~~do~~ **make** a good impression with my very first Thai meal. I think my sister ~~utterly~~ **thoroughly/really** enjoyed her birthday.

2.4

> **lead** CONTROL E /liːd/ *verb* [**I** or **T**] (**led**, **led**) to control a group of people, a country, or a situation: *I think we've chosen the right person to lead the expedition.* ○ *I've asked Gemma to lead the discussion.* ○ *Who will be leading the inquiry into the accident?*
> • **lead *sb* by the nose** *INFORMAL* to control someone and make them do exactly what you want them to do

Possible new sentences:
1 He led an expedition to the Amazon in 1887.
2 She led the discussion very skilfully.
3 The Prime Minister appointed a senior judge to lead the inquiry into the scandal.

Follow up
Here are some possible good collocations for the words suggested. You may choose to record them in different ways, of course. The important thing is that they are recorded as collocations in a phrase or sentence that will help you to understand their meaning and to remember them.
desperately ill; desperately busy; desperately keen; desperately in love with
an acute pain; a sudden pain; to relieve the pain; to put up with pain (see also Unit 3)
a wise decision; to be older and wiser; to be wise after the event; a wise guy (informal)
to run a business; to run smoothly; buses run regularly; to run for political office

Unit 3

3.1 1 It puts them **in bold**.
2 in pain, constant pain, ease the pain, a sharp pain, aches and pains
3 It can take you to a lot of information about a word or about types of word very quickly.
4 You are shown a list of other ways in which the relevant word is used.
5 By writing INFORMAL after the relevant use of the word.
6 If your dictionary does not indicate good collocations either by putting them in bold or by using them in example sentences, then you should seriously consider getting another dictionary that will help you in this way. It will be very useful when you are writing English compositions as well as helping you to improve your vocabulary.
7 Your answer will depend on your own dictionary.
8 Your answer will depend on your own dictionary.

3.2

making others experience pain	*the experience of being in pain*	*making pain go away*
to cause pain to inflict pain	to suffer pain to complain of pain to be racked with pain to feel pain to experience pain	to alleviate pain to ease pain to lessen pain to soothe pain to relieve pain pain subsides

3.3 You might find these collocations:
aches and pains
a dull ache
to have a stomach ache

Unit 4

4.1
1 a brief chat
2 bright colours
3 key issues
4 a major problem

4.2
1 launch
2 was booming
3 create
4 merge
5 poses
6 expanded

4.3
1 nostalgia
2 horror
3 anger
4 pride
5 tears
6 pride

4.4
1 blissfully
2 fully
3 proudly
4 happily
5 gently
6 softly

4.5
1 B
2 F
3 E
4 C
5 F
6 D
7 A
8 B
9 A
10 D

Unit 5

5.1
1 <u>Cyclists should dismount</u> before crossing the footbridge. (F)
2 Never <u>dispose of batteries and similar items</u> by throwing them onto a fire. (F)
3 The students were all <u>bored stiff</u> by the lecture. (I)
4 Passengers must <u>alight from the bus</u> through the rear door. (F)
5 The grass <u>badly needs</u> cutting. (I)
6 Please place all used tickets in <u>the receptacle provided</u> as you leave the building. (F)

5.2
1 slash prices, pump prices, major companies
2 detectives quiz, missing teenager, prime suspect
3 floods hit, battling against floods
4 axe (200) jobs, made redundant, job losses, falling profits

5.3 *Suggested answers:*
1 Have you heard? The oil companies are bringing down / putting down / lowering / reducing their prices.
2 Have you heard? Detectives have interrogated/questioned/interviewed a business man about the missing teenager. *or* Detectives are interrogating/questioning/interviewing ...
3 Have you heard? Floods are affecting / there are floods in the Central region.
4 Have you heard? The Presco car firm is getting rid of 200 jobs (*or* staff/people) / is making 200 workers (*or* staff/people) redundant / is laying off 200 people (*or* workers/staff).

5.4
1 We raised capital to expand the business.
2 They submitted a tender for the new stadium.
3 They went into partnership to develop a new range of products.
4 We started up a business to supply sports equipment to schools.

5.5
1 dead keen
2 boarding the aircraft
3 bore the cost of
4 dropped out of
5 launched into

Unit 6

6.1
1 deeply ashamed
2 ridiculously cheap
3 highly controversial
4 utterly stupid
5 highly successful
6 bitterly disappointing
7 strongly/utterly opposed
8 utterly ridiculous
9 ridiculously easy
10 deeply concerned

6.2
1 ridiculously cheap
2 highly controversial
3 strongly/utterly opposed
4 bitterly disappointing
5 deeply ashamed
6 highly successful
7 ridiculously easy
8 utterly stupid
9 deeply concerned
10 utterly ridiculous

6.3 *The incorrect collocations are:*
1 strongly love
2 highly exhausted
3 bitterly regard
4 absolutely tired
5 deeply successful

6.4 Everyone was complaining **bitterly** when they heard about the new plan. People were **deeply** shocked to hear that children would be **strictly** forbidden to use the sports ground and most people were strongly opposed to the new rules. Even people who normally never expressed an opinion were **utterly** appalled by the proposals.

Unit 7

7.1
1 made a mistake
2 make a decision
3 make arrangements / an arrangement
4 make a change / (some) changes to
5 make a choice
6 make a contribution

7.2
1 do
2 doing
3 make
4 do
5 make
6 do

7.3
1 do
2 do
3 make; do
4 make
5 make

Unit 8

8.1
1 They can go bald. / They can go grey.
2 You can go red.
3 Your face / You can go white. If the news is a great shock your hair might go/turn white.
4 They can go yellow.
5 They turn red.
6 John Milton went blind.
7 Beethoven went deaf.
8 Hamlet went mad.
9 It might turn grey. / It might go dark.

8.2 1 Dinosaurs **became** extinct ...
2 ... I'd like to **have** lots of children.
3 Janet **became** depressed ...
4 ... dreamt of **becoming** famous.
5 Would you be interested in **becoming** involved ...
6 More people have **become** homeless ...
7 My sister **had** a baby ...
8 My grandfather **had/suffered** a heart attack ...

8.3 As you **grow** older, you'll begin to understand your parents better. **Becoming** angry with them all the time doesn't help. You may not want to go to summer camp when none of your friends will be there, but your parents know you will soon **make** new friends there. You would all have gone on a family holiday together if your grandmother hadn't **fallen** ill, but surely you can understand why they don't want to leave her. You'll feel much more sympathetic to your parents' feelings when you **have** a child of your own!

8.4

1 mad	5 fell
2 turned	6 grew
3 gone	7 falling
4 going / to go	8 went/turned

Unit 9

9.1 *Suggested questions:*
1 Could you have a look at this letter before I send it?
2 Did you have an argument / a row?
3 What happened? Did you have an accident?
4 How was the holiday? Did you have fun / have a good time?
5 Shall we have a break for half an hour or so?
6 Nice bike! Can I have a go/try (on it)?
7 When you're free, could I have a chat with you about next year?
8 What's the matter? Are you having difficulty / problems / a problem reading it?

9.2

1 paid	7 had
2 took	8 pay
3 paid	9 take
4 had	10 have
5 paid	11 take
6 took	12 had

9.3 Next time you **take** a trip to the coast, why not **take** the train?
Why suffer endless delays in long traffic jams? And why **take** risks when you're travelling – **take** a train and arrive safely. What's more, if you decide to **take** a holiday in the capital city, you'll have a more relaxing time if you **take** a train. Or why not pay a surprise visit to an old friend during an off-peak time? Call now and **take advantage of** our special offers. 0800347655

Unit 10

10.1

1 close	5 close
2 start	6 began
3 large	7 big
4 finished; end	8 end

10.2
1 solitary
2 antique
3 only
4 sole
5 ancient
6 alone
7 lonely
8 old
9 single [*elderly parents* is also a possible collocation]
10 elderly

10.3
1 Were many people **injured** in the earthquake?
2 Single parents **raising** children without a partner's support are entitled to financial help from the government
3 My mobile isn't working. I need to **charge** the battery.
4 She has a lot of beautiful **antique** jewellery.
5 When we moved house, two men helped us to **load** the van.
6 That's not news – it's **ancient** history!
7 I don't know how to **load** a gun, let alone fire one.
8 I've never been very successful at **growing** plants.

10.4 *Possible answers:*
1 They're loading a ship.
2 She's growing plants.
3 He's studying ancient history.
4 The chair is damaged.
5 He's raising sheep.
6 He has injured his leg. *or* He is injured.

Follow-up
Possible collocations:
big city, house, eater, sister, brother, difference, day, deal, idea, business – when *big* means *important*, it cannot be replaced by *large*.
large – large city, large house, large number, large survey, large intestine

Unit 11

11.1
1 earn/make
2 gained
3 won
4 achieve
5 made
6 beat/defeated, won
7 earns
8 gained

11.2
1 The woman is wearing a coat.
2 She's carrying an umbrella and a mobile phone.
3 She's using her mobile phone.
4 The man is wearing a suit.
5 He's carrying a briefcase and an umbrella.
6 He's using his umbrella.

11.3 Last year I got a new job and started **earning/making** a lot more money. I realised I could afford to **spend** more money on my holiday than I usually do and decided to **spend** a month in Australia. I knew it would be hot there and so I wouldn't need to **take** warm clothes with me. In fact, I **wore** a t-shirt and jeans all the time I was there. I **wore** a hat all the time too, of course, to protect me from the sun. It was fantastic there. I **spent** a week sightseeing in Sydney and then **spent** the rest of the time travelling round the country. I even **achieved** my lifelong ambition of stroking a koala.

11.4
1 The Democratic Party **won** the election.
2 The ruling power **has gained** control of the situation.
3 Our team **won** the match.
4 I **earned/made** a lot of money last month.
5 Our company made **a profit** last year.

11.5
1 Where did you **spend** your last holiday?
2 How much money did you **earn/make** last week?
3 What do you always **carry/take** with you when you go out?
4 Have you ever **won** a trophy?
5 What aim would you particularly like to **achieve** in life?

Possible answers:
1 I spent my last holiday in Switzerland.
2 I'm not sure what I earned last week – much the same as usual, probably.
3 I always carry my mobile phone, some money, a credit card and my keys.
4 I once won a trophy for writing an essay at school.
5 I'd like to achieve my aim of writing a novel.

Unit 12

12.1

1 sunny	4 dark
2 lit up	5 were shining / shone
3 lighten	6 darkened

12.2

1 Paula	4 Emma (and Helena)
2 Rob	5 Thomas
3 Yvonne	6 Jason

12.3
1 My cheeks were burning with embarrassment.
2 Violence has flared up in the capital city.
3 The ideas flowed during the discussion.
4 The famous footballer's divorce was surrounded by a blaze of publicity.

12.4 1 b 2 b 3 a 4 c

12.5 *Possible answers:*
1 a bright future [a future that is looking happy and successful]
a bright child [an intelligent child]
2 a warm welcome [a friendly welcome]
a warm smile [a friendly smile]
3 cold eyes [unfriendly eyes]
a cold stare [an unfriendly stare]

Unit 13

13.1
1 snow
2 fog/mist
3 winds/sun
4 wind
5 frost
6 rain
7 sunshine – Note that you can also talk about **unbroken cloud**.
8 fog/mist – Note that you can also talk about **a blanket of snow**.

13.2

1 strong	4 freezing cold
2 wind died down	5 heavy/driving
3 deteriorate / get worse	6 lifted

13.3 I wish I'd worn a warmer jacket. There's a **freezing cold / biting** wind. At least it's not **pouring with rain** today. I got **soaked to the skin** yesterday. I wish I was **soaking up the sunshine** on a Mediterranean beach.

13.4
1 Very heavy rain or snow melting perhaps.
2 You can probably see heavy grey clouds – but note that it has not started to rain yet.
3 It's unexpected, unusual for the time of year or the place, and unusually strong.
4 It's probably harder to drive if there is dense fog. However, patches of fog can also be dangerous as you may unexpectedly run into fog.
5 Heavy rain with wind.
6 An image of violence is created.
7 People can blow or whistle. They do this by exhaling air from their lips. So you might blow on soup or tea to cool it. If you whistle you make a noise by blowing through your lips in a special way.
8 *Devastated* suggests most destruction and *damaged* suggests least destruction.

13.5 Other collocations you might have found are:

wind	**rain**	**snow**
not a breath of wind	light rain	snow falls
a gust of wind	a downpour of rain	snow melts
	a shower of rain	a blanket of snow
	to rain hard	
	rain fell heavily	

Unit 14

14.1

1 travel	6 journey
2 trip	7 trips
3 journey	8 travel/trips
4 travel	9 travel
5 trip	10 journey

14.2

1 make; fully	5 fasten
2 aisle; window	6 board
3 connecting	7 run
4 entertainment	8 smart/luxury; accommodation

14.3
1 A bumpy flight.
2 Most people prefer smooth flights – though some people perhaps enjoy it when it is bumpy because it is more exciting!
3 A scheduled flight.
4 In-flight magazines.
5 A business trip is one specific journey for business purposes whereas business travel refers to travelling in general for business purposes.
6 Return journey.
7 Not necessarily – family-run means that the main hotel staff are largely from the same family.

14.4 *Possible answer based on the experience of one of the authors:*

Last year I went to California. I made all the travel arrangements myself over the Internet so it was cheaper than using a travel agent. I got a charter flight and good budget accommodation in San Francisco for a few nights. Although it was a long, tiring journey from London, it was worth it. While in San Francisco, I took a day trip to the other side of the Bay, across the Golden Gate Bridge, and also went on a boat trip, which was fun. I had a smooth flight on the return journey but I was exhausted when I got home.

Unit 15

15.1 1 fell into; open 2 followed; covered 3 dense forest

15.2 A chain of **snow-covered** mountains runs down the east of the country. The Wassa River, the country's biggest, **winds/flows** slowly from the northern mountains to the sea. Even in summer it is a **bleak** landscape, with its dark, **rocky** mountains and its cold streams. But for me it is the **familiar** landscape of my childhood and I am happy that the government has decided to **protect** this environment. It is a dramatic **setting** which is **well** worth visiting for anyone who likes **spectacular** views.

15.3
1 took
2 turned; caught
3 sandy; stretched
4 blocks

15.4

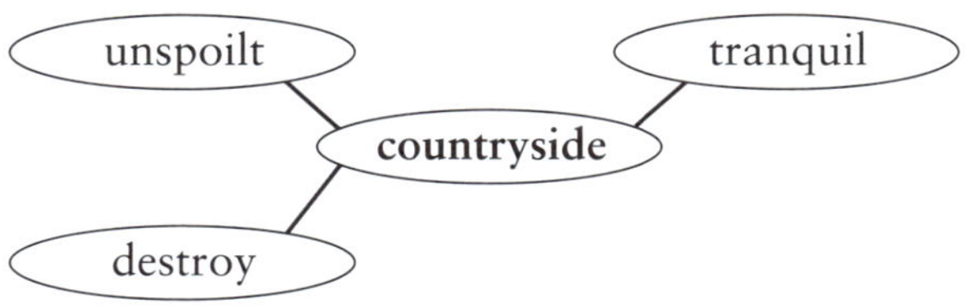

15.5
1 surrounding countryside
2 dominates the landscape; panoramic view
3 secluded beaches
4 breathtaking scenery
5 uninterrupted views

Unit 16

16.1
1 high-rise flats
2 a tree-lined avenue
3 a city skyline
4 quaint old buildings (on a cobbled street)

16.2

positive	**negative**
relaxed atmosphere	over-priced restaurants
lively bar	urban wasteland
imposing building	no-go area
fashionable club	shanty town
	run-down buildings

16.3
1 the incessant roar of the traffic
2 (the volume of) traffic
3 an over-priced restaurant
4 a shanty town
5 a conservation area
6 a pricey restaurant
7 high-rise flats
8 quaint

16.4
1 It is a sprawling city covering an enormous area.
2 It is full of upmarket shops, which are too expensive for me.
3 There was bumper-to-bumper traffic all the way to the airport.
4 I get asthma from the terrible exhaust fumes in the city centre.
5 I live in a residential area but work in the city centre.
6 Some of the more deprived areas are not far from the city centre.
7 The main street in town runs from the castle to the river.
8 The main street is lined with shops and cafés.
9 On the outskirts are some industrial zones and some large supermarkets.
10 The streets were strewn with litter.

Unit 17

17.1 These collocations clearly describe negative aspects of character:
a selfish streak
bear a grudge
make a fool out of someone
hurt someone's feelings

These collocations may describe negative aspects of character – it depends on your point of view:
painfully shy
snap decisions
brutally honest

17.2
1 I know that I **have** a tendency to **bear** a grudge, but I just can't forget something bad a friend did to me recently. She has a selfish **streak** and doesn't care sometimes how much she **hurts** my feelings. I am finding it increasingly hard to **keep** my temper with her. But perhaps it might be better to **lose** my temper and let her know how I really feel?
2 I have always tried to **put** others first and not to think of myself. I believe you should not lose your **patience** with your friends, but if someone seems to enjoy **making** a fool out of you in front of other people, do those rules of friendship still apply?
3 I'm a little shy, though not **painfully** shy, but sometimes I think I **give** the impression that I'm unfriendly. How can I convince people that I'm good **company** and worth getting to know?
4 Should I talk about personal matters to my closest colleague at work? She is not very good at **keeping** secrets and she has a very **vivid** imagination. She always promises not to tell other people, but I'm not sure she always **keeps** her word.
5 My boyfriend has a really friendly, **outgoing** personality and a great **sense** of humour. He's **highly** intelligent and has a **razor**-sharp mind. The perfect man. We've been together now for a year, and I like him a lot, but don't *love* him any more. Should I be **brutally** honest with him and tell him?
6 I think a friend is destroying himself with drugs. I feel a **sense** of responsibility towards him. He has always been **fiercely** loyal to me in good and bad times, which is a wonderful **aspect** of his personality. I feel I ought to contact the police or social services, but I don't want to make a **snap** decision which I'll regret later.

17.3
1 B: Yes, he's found it hard **to come to terms** with his new situation.
2 B: No, it's true. He just can't **take a joke**, can he?
3 B: Yes, it certainly **revealed her true character**.
4 B: Yes, she always **sets high standards for herself**.
5 B: Well, two-year-olds often **throw tantrums**.

17.4 Other collocations you might find are:
1 to give your word; a man or woman of his or her word
2 to have a bad/foul temper; to have a sweet temper; to control your temper; tempers got frayed
3 sense of duty; sense of honour; sense of fun

Unit 18

18.1

'fat' words	'thin' words
portly	lanky
dumpy	slender
chubby	slim

1 slender, slim
2 lanky
3 chubby
4 portly
5 dumpy

18.2

bushy eyebrows
tiny tot
oval face
striking resemblance
broad shoulders
droopy moustache
chubby cheeks
dishevelled hair

18.3

1 tiny tot
2 immaculately groomed
3 jet-black
4 shoulder-length
5 lovely complexion
6 striking appearance
7 slim/slender waist
8 portly gentleman
9 youthful appearance
10 gone
11 go

18.4

1 fair; dark
2 upturned; straight
3 round; pointed
4 coarse; sleek

Unit 19

19.1

1 extended
2 confirmed
3 distant
4 close-knit
5 dysfunctional
6 late
7 broken

19.2 Charles and I are hoping to **start** a family soon. We both want to **have** lots of children. Ideally, I'd like to have my first baby next year, when I'll be 25. My sister is **expecting** a baby now. It's **due** next month. She's going to be a **single** parent and it'll be hard for her to **bring up / raise** a child on her own.

19.3

1 apply for custody
2 get a divorce
3 estranged wife
4 nuclear family
5 provide for your family
6 distant cousin
7 set up home
8 trial separation

19.4 *Possible answers:*

1 Just my husband and son.
2 No, I don't know much at all about my distant relatives.
3 In a small flat in London.
4 A stable home, where there are not likely to be sudden or unpleasant changes. A *deprived home* is one where living conditions are extremely poor.
5 to be expecting a baby
6 Yes, they can. A respectable family is one that outwardly conforms to social norms, but within its own private world, it may be dysfunctional. The British Royal Family is often referred to as dysfunctional even though most people consider it to be respectable.
7 ex-
8 grant custody

19.5 If possible, ask your teacher or another good speaker of English to correct your paragraph for you.

Unit 20

20.1

1 make
2 have
3 striking
4 spoil
5 mutual
6 form
7 acquaintance
8 grew

20.2 special friends
make a commitment
accept a proposal
return someone's love
have an affair
keep in contact
lose contact
strike up a friendship
love at first sight

20.3
1 grow
2 to be/fall madly in love
3 accept a proposal
4 close friends
5 keep in touch with

20.4 The gaps can be filled in the following ways. The answers are, of course, private and personal!
1 sight
2 make
3 fell
4 life
5 returned
6 have

20.5 *Possible collocations:*

love
to make love
to love someone deeply
to send someone your love

friend
my best friend
an old friend
a childhood friend
a true friend

friendship
a lasting friendship
to hold out the hand of friendship
to value someone's friendship

relationship
a good relationship
to end a relationship
a family relationship

Unit 21

21.1
1 I was bitterly/deeply/hugely disappointed.
2 Jess is a highly emotional individual.
3 She felt desperately sad.
4 Her childhood was blissfully happy.
5 I was worried sick.
6 She felt deeply depressed.

21.2

Delete Reply Reply All Forward Print

1 Dear James
I have to tell you that there is widespread condemnation and mounting anger over the news that the company pension scheme is to be closed down. The issue has aroused strong feelings among the staff. I am personally becoming increasingly anxious that the situation might get out of control, and ask you to act immediately.
With best wishes,
Joanne Withers
Staff representative

2 Dear Joanne,
I too am seething with anger over this pension question. I tried to express my disappointment over it to the Board, but they simply dismissed the issue and that just made me extremely angry. I feel badly let down. I shall continue to do what I can.
Yours sincerely
James Horgan (Resource Manager)

3 Gareth,
You probably know I didn't get the job I applied for. It's a huge disappointment.
Christina

4 Dear Winston,
I felt a great sadness when I heard of Patrick's death.
Will you be going to the funeral? It will be such a sad occasion, won't it?
Pamela

21.3
1 Examples could be a wedding, the birth of a healthy child, a degree ceremony, a birthday or other celebration.
2 a/the happy couple
3 lasting happiness
4 emotional **impact**
5 I was worried sick

Follow up
The Cambridge University Press website dictionary search will show you *keep your temper*, *quick temper*, *be in a bad/foul temper*, then if you click again on *temper (BEHAVIOUR)*, you will find *have a real temper*, *even-tempered* and *bad-tempered*.

Unit 22

22.1
1 fully-furnished accommodation
2 short-let accommodation
3 a residential area
4 a studio flat
5 off-road parking
6 a fully-fitted kitchen

22.2
1 We want to turn our garage into a granny flat.
2 Jill has invited me to her house-warming party.
3 Next week I have to move out of my flat.
4 Karl makes a business out of doing up old houses.
5 Our bedroom overlooks the garden.
6 Our house needs to be completely refurbished.
7 I hope that one day I'll have a place of my own.
8 The bank can help if you want to take out a mortgage.

22.3
1 We live on a busy road, but we're lucky because we have off-road **parking.**
2 Gemma has moved **out of** her old flat and has now got a new place in Walville Street.
3 We're building an **extension** to our house which will give us a bigger kitchen.
4 The flat is **fully** furnished, which is good because I have no furniture of my own.
5 She had to **take** out a big mortgage as the house was very expensive.
6 There is no **affordable** housing for young people in this area; prices are ridiculously high.
7 New people have **moved** into the house next door. I haven't met them yet.
8 It's a very **spacious** apartment with a huge living room and a big kitchen.
9 The flat is **available** to rent from the first of March onwards.
10 My brother and his wife live in a **draughty** old cottage.

22.4
Your dream home could be waiting for you at Highdale Cottages. All cottages **have a view of** the River Marn. Ideal for anyone seeking a **second home** in the area. Telephone 3340251 for appointments to view

22.5
1 … welcome her home.
2 … leave home / move out.
3 … feel at home.
4 … make yourself at home.
5 … feel homesick.

Unit 23

23.1
1 set menu
2 food additives
3 junk food
4 ready meals
5 fresh produce (**Fresh food** is also a possible collocation.)

23.2
1 Food additives
2 Junk food
3 ready meals
4 fresh produce
5 set menu

23.3

1 Suzie	4 Nina
2 Ken	5 Polly
3 Richard	6 Archie

23.4
1 **Processed foods** may damage our health in the long term.
2 Some people always have three **square meals** a day, but I prefer a **hearty breakfast** and then a **light meal** around midday and a more **substantial meal** in the evening.
3 There are some overpriced restaurants in the city centre, but down at the beach, there are some nice, **reasonably priced** ones.
4 On my birthday my parents took me out for a **slap-up meal**. They wanted to go for a **gourmet meal** but I said I'd prefer something more ordinary.
5 Ice tea is a **refreshing drink** on a hot day, and is probably better for you than **soft drinks** such as cola or lemonade.
6 Let me take you out to dinner on your birthday. Or would you prefer a **home-cooked meal**? I could make dinner for you at my place.

Unit 24

24.1
Matthew: Have you read that new book that has just **come out** about Ireland?
Lorna: No, I don't go to bookshops and I don't read **book reviews**. What's it about?
Matthew: Well, it **deals with** the Irish War of Independence. It's very authentic and it manages to **capture the atmosphere** of Ireland at the beginning of the 20th century.
Lorna: Is it just historical facts, then?
Matthew: No, the **central characters** are two brothers who have different opinions about the war and this divides their family. In the **opening chapters** they're happy and do everything together, but by the **closing chapter** they have become enemies.
Lorna: Mm, it sounds a bit depressing to me.
Matthew: Well, it certainly doesn't **have a happy ending**, but I liked it, and it's **highly recommended** by all the critics.
Lorna: So, a book with a pleasant **beginning** and a sad **end(ing)**. Not for me, I'm afraid. I prefer the opposite.

24.2

Across	Down
3 absorbed	1 cameo
5 engrossed	2 nominated
6 stage	4 effects
7 lead	

24.3
full house
bedtime reading
box-office hit
big screen
female lead

24.4

1 film	3 book/magazine/article
2 (library) book	4 reading

Unit 25

25.1
1 The band's last CD was a **massive/big** hit.
2 There are some great **up-tempo** numbers on this new CD.
3 The band has a **huge** following of dedicated fans.
4 Music was **blasting out from** a CD player when I entered the house.
5 She gave a **virtuoso** performance of Heder's violin concerto last night.

25.2

1 ~~likers~~	lovers	5 ~~comprise~~	feature
2 ~~published~~	released	6 ~~control~~	capture
3 ~~got solo~~	went solo	7 ~~living~~	live
4 ~~inheritance~~	heritage	8 ~~makes a~~	goes on

25.3

1 background music
2 easy listening
3 a pop idol
4 a rap artist
5 to tune an instrument
6 to strum (a guitar)

25.4

1 adoring
2 performance
3 catchy
4 take up
5 haunting
6 talent

Unit 26

26.1

You can **do** judo!
You can **go** swimming!
You can **do** circuit training!
You can **go** skate-boarding!
You can **play** badminton!
You can **do** weight lifting!
You can **play** table tennis!
You can even **play** darts!
In fact, you can **do/play** almost any sport you can think of. So join now!

26.2

personal best
blow a whistle
bring on a substitute
fail a drugs test
enter a competition
set a record
achieve your ambitions
train hard
enhance your performance
take the lead (*take a drugs test* is also possible)

26.3

Hi, Jose,
Do you fancy coming on a sporting weekend with me next month? It sounds great – would make a change from playing computer games. You can **do** lots of different activities. You could even **go** fishing, I think. You can't go skiing at this time of year but you can **go** water skiing, if you like. Everyone has to **do** general exercises first thing in the morning and then you can **do/play** whatever sport you like, more or less. I've never **played** badminton so I think I'm going to do that. Then in the afternoon I'm looking forward to the chance to practise my tennis serve with their professional coach. Please try to come!
Giorgio

26.4

1 win
2 fight
3 deserved
4 tackling
5 possession
6 gained
7 stage/round
8 competition
9 set (possibly *beat*, if there was an existing record for a team with several family members in it)

Unit 27

27.1

1 sustain minor injuries
2 contract typhoid
3 have an attack of diarrhoea
4 develop breast cancer
5 be diagnosed with autism / breast cancer
6 catch a cold

27.2 *Suggested answers:*

1 **develop** arthritis
2 **had/suffered/experienced** moderate or severe **attacks of** diarrhoea
3 To **be diagnosed with** cancer
4 **contract** malaria
5 **sustained** serious injuries
6 **catch** pneumonia

27.3

1 serious; life-threatening
2 terminally
3 dull
4 balanced
5 splitting
6 trivial
7 stick; shape
8 incurable
9 taken; excruciating
10 healthy; vigorous
11 prescribed; alleviate
12 slight

Unit 28

28.1 The strongest collocations are the following, although others, such as **enter a chatroom** or **visit a website** are also possible.

1 browse the web
2 be connected to the Internet
3 enter the web address
4 access a website
5 compose a message
6 attach a file
7 go online
8 visit a chat room
9 select an option

28.2

1 maintained
2 connected
3 receive
4 navigate
5 burn
6 hard
7 delete
8 online

28.3 *Possible answers:*

1 re-install the programs
2 save / back up your work
3 delete or erase a file
4 that you have put in the correct address
5 a search engine
6 The e-mail will bounce.
7 Hit 'reply', compose your message and then press 'send'.
8 download the picture
9 forward the message
10 send an attachment / send it as an attachment
11 to your home address
12 predictive text

28.4

1 ring
2 connection
3 held
4 hacked
5 access
6 clip
7 images
8 select / click on

Unit 29

29.1 I have three daughters. The oldest one **studied for / took** a degree in economics at Birmingham University. She **obtained / was awarded** her bachelor's degree last year and is now **carrying out / conducting** some research on taxation laws in different countries. The second one is **taking / enrolled on** a course at Newcastle University. She's **studying/taking** history. She loves it, though she says she has to **write** far too many assignments. My youngest daughter is still at school. She's **sitting/taking** her school-leaving exams in the summer. She'll go to university next year if she **receives / is given** good enough grades in her exams. She wants to **study/take** sociology and then **obtain/acquire** a social work qualification. My daughters are all **receiving** a much better education than I ever had.

29.2

1 do	6 held
2 take/sit	7 draft
3 hand/give	8 assessment
4 giving/doing	9 go
5 withdraw	10 provide/give/offer

29.3

1 passed	5 complete
2 give	6 send
3 recognises	7 leave
4 attend	8 keep

29.4 *Possible answers:*

1 Schoolchildren often take those exams at about 16 if they are leaving school as soon as possible, or at 18 if they are planning to go on to further or higher education.
2 about 6 years
3 It does not depend on how you are feeling on one specific day. You can see whether you are improving or not as you go along. You can spend more time doing your work.
4 Feedback on the clarity and accuracy of the presentation, on the student's pronunciation, on the student's use of visual aids.
5 It helps you revise what you did in class. It gives you a chance to do extra things that you don't have time to do in class.
6 Write the words down in context, and revise what you've written down every few days or weeks.
7 Further education is less academic than higher or tertiary education. Students studying, say, car mechanics or secretarial skills are in further education whereas students studying, say, to be lawyers or doctors are in higher or tertiary education.
8 You'd expect a final draft to be better than a first draft, to be better organised, to have fewer spelling mistakes, and so on.

Unit 30

30.1

1 work	5 work
2 career	6 career
3 career	7 job
4 job	8 career; job; career

30.2 *Suggested answer:*

applicant	*1–3*	*reasons*
Kevin Marsh	3	Too young, does not have any experience
Nurdan Ozbek	1	Enough experience, right qualifications, has worked in a team, short notice
Nuala Riley	2	Wrong kind of experience, long period of notice, person needed immediately

30.3

1 She has set some difficult targets for us all.
2 We're making preparations for the sales conference.
3 I always keep my appointments.
4 Jane will take the minutes at the meeting.
5 I have to give a presentation to my colleagues.
6 He never achieved his goals in his career.
7 He fielded my phone calls while I took time off.

30.4 **dead-end job** – a job that has few prospects of leading somewhere interesting or successful
glittering career – an impressive career, one that is admired by many people
career spanning – a career covering a specified and notably long period of time
lucrative job – a job where the person earns a lot of money for doing the work
rewarding job – a job where the person gets a lot of personal satisfaction – emotional rather than financial – from doing the work

Unit 31

31.1
1 float
2 launch
3 make
4 go
5 go
6 go
7 carry out / conduct
8 go
9 set
10 make

31.2
1 d
2 b
3 f
4 a
5 c
6 e

31.3
1 value
2 win; stiff
3 run
4 doing
5 turnover
6 balance
7 bid
8 brisk

31.4
1 runs
2 up
3 does
4 made
5 figures
6 business
7 won
8 competition
9 put
10 rival
11 struck/done
12 create
13 secret
14 service

Unit 32

32.1 You may be able to justify other answers than those offered here.
1 **Groundbreaking research, makes a significant contribution to, powerful arguments** and **shape our thinking** all suggest that the writer admires Georgescu's work.
2 **Strenuously defends** and **come under attack** both suggest that Partridge's work has been criticised.
3 **Gives an account of, provides evidence** and **concise summary** all suggest that Marina Kass presents facts.
4 **Establish a connection** and **significant trends** both suggest that Nathan Peel is interested in analysing social statistics.

32.2
1 The example of Mrs Brown **is/provides a clear illustration** of the need for better medical services in the area.
2 A doctoral thesis must always **acknowledge its sources.**
3 Dr Kahn's results offer/provide **irrefutable proof** that our theory is correct.
4 The article begins **with a concise summary of** the background to the research.
5 The book **gives an interesting account of** the life of Marx as a young man.
6 Janet's theory has **come under attack** recently in a number of journals.

32.3 *Suggested answers:*
groundbreaking research
makes a significant contribution to
powerful arguments
shape our thinking
strenuously defends
played a central role
goes into great detail
concise summary
irrefutable proof
significant trends

32.4
1 play a part
2 set out an argument
3 convinced by someone's argument
4 come under attack
5 make a contribution
6 carry out a study
7 go into detail
8 shape people's thinking

32.5
1 powerful
2 supporting
3 tendency
4 challenge
5 groundbreaking
6 shape

32.6 *Possible answers – there are many other ways of completing this table:*

verb	*adjective*	*noun*
to publish	*an outstanding*	article
to carry out	original	research
to conduct	a controlled	experiment
to develop	a coherent	theory
to undertake	a comprehensive	survey

Unit 33

33.1
1 fall
2 distinction
3 take
4 raise
5 making
6 case
7 touch

33.2
1 assess
2 convincingly
3 draw
4 lend
5 forward
6 hold
7 draw
8 lay
9 profoundly
10 draw

33.3
1 presents
2 suggests
3 adopts
4 states
5 briefly
6 draws
7 hold
8 raises

33.4 Kerr takes **up** a controversial position in his latest article. He **puts** forward the argument that differences in behaviour between the sexes can be explained totally by the genes. He attempts to **make** a case for educating boys and girls separately in their primary school years. He argues, occasionally **convincingly**, that both sexes would benefit from this. He **draws** attention to recent research which, he claims, **lends** support **to** his argument. However, he fails to **take** a number of important factors into consideration. He also **makes** no reference to the important work of Potter and Sinclair in this field. I am sure that I will not be alone in disagreeing **profoundly** with many of his conclusions.

Follow up
Possible collocations are:
revolutionary theory, dismiss/disprove someone's theory
groundbreaking research, a major research project
present one's argument, a powerful argument

Unit 34

34.1

1 obey/observe
2 observe/obey
3 break
4 respect
5 act
6 passing/introducing
7 introducing/passing
8 upholding/enforcing
9 enforcing/upholding

34.2

1 The rules apply to all students in the college.
2 The rules prohibit the use of mobile phones in class.
3 The rules allow students to book college guestrooms at weekends.
4 The regulations stipulate that coursework must be handed in on time.
5 Most students follow the rules without too many complaints.
6 The authorities bent the rules to allow Mary to submit her coursework a little late.
7 All students must comply with the regulations.

34.3

1 e) Bill Sikes robs a bank.
2 g) The police carry out an investigation.
3 b) Bill Sikes goes on trial.
4 a) A number of witnesses appear in court.
5 f) The jury reaches its verdict.
6 c) Bill Sikes is found guilty.
7 d) Bill Sikes is severely punished.

34.4

1 to win his or her case
2 a fair trial
3 carry out an investigation
4 They may face the death penalty.
5 It might act as a deterrent.
6 reach a verdict
7 harsh punishments/sentences
8 a heavy fine

34.5

1 Everyone must comply with these regulations.
2 These rules apply to all citizens.
3 The jury reached a verdict of guilty.
4 The police are carrying out an investigation into the bank robbery.
5 Our company always acts within the law.
6 The rules do not allow students to eat and drink in the classrooms.

Unit 35

35.1

1 a young/juvenile offender
2 a convicted criminal
3 a hardened criminal
4 to serve a sentence
5 to commit a crime / an offence
6 a political prisoner
7 a common criminal
8 a criminal record

35.2

1 b
2 f
3 e
4 c
5 a
6 d

35.3

1 committed
2 breaking
3 stealing
4 offenders
5 spate
6 tackle/combat
7 fight
8 juvenile

35.4

1 Worried, because it would mean that a lot of crimes were currently being committed in the area.
2 A crime that is not too serious, for example, small-scale shoplifting or putting graffiti on public places.
3 They are putting a lot of time and money into solving serious crime.
4 combat
5 a crime in which innocent people are killed for political purposes
6 robberies – *a spate of* is used to describe a series of negative events
7 For example breaking windows, damaging telephone boxes, breaking down fences, slashing car tyres, etc.

Unit 36

36.1

Monday	latest
Tuesday	make
Wednesday	headline/front-page
Thursday	leaked
Friday	hit; ran
Saturday	front-page
Sunday	hold

36.2

Across	**Down**
1 down	2 plans
4 go	3 flick
6 close	5 item
7 break	

36.3

1 turn; keep; comes
2 seized; taken
3 struck; caught
4 hold; interested
5 top; controversial
6 launched

Unit 37

37.1 1 Marianne 2 Catherine 3 Briony 4 Philip 5 Anthony

37.2 1 soared 2 ridiculous/low price 3 reasonably priced 4 rock-bottom/ridiculous 5 went; go up / rise

37.3 1 make 2 making; steady 3 tight 4 going; short 5 raise 6 small; tied up 7 big; seriously

Unit 38

38.1 1 go; avert 2 raged; opened 3 fight 4 join(ed); horrors

38.2
1 The war between Adverbia and Collocania **broke out** in 1983 after a dispute over territory in the northern province. At first there were just **minor incidents** but it soon turned into **all-out war**. The war ended after **a decisive battle** in 1987.
2 There was **fierce fighting** in the capital city yesterday. United Nations **peacekeeping forces** are expected to enter the city as soon as **a ceasefire is called.**
3 Forces sent in to **keep the peace** in the troubled region of Phrasalia had to **withdraw/retreat** after they came **within (firing) range** of rebel artillery.
4 The Sornak Republic today **declared war** against Hobrania.
5 Armed troops were sent in to **restore order** after the riots and violence of last week.
6 Even though the two sides **signed a peace treaty / peace agreement** last July, fighting has started again and hopes for **a lasting peace** are fading.
7 As more of our soldiers were killed or **taken prisoner**, **peace activists** organised demonstrations against the unpopular war.
8 Representatives of the two sides are meeting in Zurich in an attempt to **bring about peace** in the troubled region. It is hoped that they will **negotiate a peace agreement** which both governments can accept.

38.3
1 ... a running battle ...
2 ... losing the battle ...
3 ... put up a heroic fight ...
4 ... offered no resistance ...
5 ... fighting for (his) life ...

38.4 *Possible answers:*

army – an army advances, marches, retreats; to mobilise an army; a victorious army
soldier – veteran solider; rank-and-file soldier; a wounded soldier; to serve as a soldier
battle – a fierce battle; a battle of words; a battle of wits; to go into battle; to win/lose a battle
weapon – deadly weapon; chemical weapon; biological weapon; to carry a weapon
to fight – to fight bravely; to fight bitterly; to fight hard
peace – to make peace; the peace process; a peace conference; to take part in a peace demonstration

Unit 39

39.1

1 seekers
2 layer
3 breed
4 gases
5 opportunity
6 sleep
7 death
8 need
9 lift
10 line (People can also be **on the poverty line** or **above the poverty line.**)

39.2

1 c
2 e
3 a
4 d
5 b

39.3

1 green
2 hit
3 debt
4 developing
5 margins
6 solution
7 alleviate/eradicate

39.4 *Possible answers:*

1 People may suffer from famine. Prices for food will rise.
2 petrol, diesel, coal
3 flood, earthquake, volcanic eruption, forest fire
4 It might destroy people's homes and workplaces, damage or destroy crops, destroy roads and therefore make the area inaccessible, cause diseases because of lack of clean water.
5 They could send relief teams, send essential supplies, food, medicines, etc.
6 ecological issues
7 Climate change leading to the melting of the polar ice caps.
8 Because there are more and more cars and other vehicles emitting exhaust fumes.

Unit 40

40.1

1 spare/leisure/free
2 spend
3 take
4 Make
5 killing
6 waste
7 save
8 bang/dead/right
9 tell

40.2

1 … ran out of time.
2 … worth your while.
3 … from dawn till dusk.
4 … what the future holds …
5 Did you have a good time …
6 I didn't have time to do the ironing …

40.3

1 Sally: Well, we'd better all **set our alarms**.
2 Inez: Yes. It was fantastic. I had **the time of my life**.
3 Mark: Yes, I think you learn to respect them more as **time goes by**.
4 Mary: Yes. I'll try to come and see you in the **not too distant future**.
5 Andy: Yes. I didn't wake up. The alarm didn't **go off**.
6 Teresa: Yes, she always stays up working until **the small hours**.

40.4 *Possible answers – you may well find other good collocations for these words:*

day	**clock**
day breaks	a clock strikes
day dawns	a clock chimes
at the end of the day	to watch the clock
the good old days	put the clock back/forward
in this day and age	stop the clock
hour	**minute**
last an hour	minutes tick by
with every passing hour	can you spare a minute
to work anti-social hours	do you have a minute
to work regular hours	hold on a minute
to sleep for eight solid hours	the minute something happens

Unit 41

41.1
1 babbling
2 singing
3 patter
4 an eerie
5 broken
6 rang

41.2
1 L
2 S
3 L
4 S
5 L
6 L
7 L
8 L
9 S
10 S
11 S
12 S

41.3
1 e
2 g
3 a
4 h
5 b
6 d
7 f
8 c

41.4
1 A person falling out of bed onto a carpeted floor in the room above you – something metal on stone would make a sharp noise rather than a dull thud.
2 Primary schoolchildren – as *shrill* suggests high-pitched voices.
3 Big waves – as *crashing* suggests a big sound.
4 From a bird.
5 A group of motorbikes roaring past. A large waterfall will make a loud noise but it won't be as sudden or as unpleasant as it would need to be in order to be called ear-splitting.

Unit 42

42.1
1 neighbouring
2 cover; considerable
3 far; off
4 walking; close

42.2

Although we had a ~~little~~ increase in our pay last month, we still earn very ~~small~~ wages. We have not had a ~~big~~ deal of help from the union, and ~~tall~~ prices mean that life is not easy. Luckily, we only have a ~~small~~ level of inflation at the moment.	small low great high low

42.3
1 **major** difficulties
2 **high** heels
3 on a **large** scale
4 **high** interest rates
5 **slim** book
6 **large** quantities
7 **little** brother
8 **taller** than

42.4
1 painfully
2 No (a fat book, or a plump person)
3 high tide
4 tall
5 little
6 deal
7 small
8 No. We'd say, 'Could you help me do some little things before dinner?'
9 You'd prefer low interest rates (not high interest rates) because then you wouldn't need to pay so much extra money back to the bank.

Unit 43

43.1
1 bright colours; subdued colours
2 colours go
3 colour ran
4 colours clash
5 touch of colour
6 colour fades

43.2
1 a candle flickers
2 a beam of light
3 pitch dark
4 a faint glow
5 a star twinkles
6 pale green
7 green issues
8 a grey area
9 cast a shadow
10 blacken someone's name

43.3
1 The police are looking for someone who can **shed light on** how the accident happened.
2 He has always been **under the shadow of** his world-famous father.
3 In the east the sky **was tinged with gold**.
4 Joe's crazy behaviour certainly **adds colour** to our dull office.
5 **The glare of the sun** can make driving difficult at this time of day.
6 She walked until the fire was just a **pinpoint of light** in the distance.
7 It was **growing dark** and Jill began to feel a little afraid.
8 The newspapers seem to be trying to **blacken** the minister's **name**.

43.4
1 A draught, the wind or some other movement of air.
2 A ray of sunlight.
3 The night. If you want to say that someone's hair is very black, you would call it jet black.
4 Far away, because *a faint glow* means that the light is not strong.
5 *A star shines* suggests a more constant strong light, whereas *a star twinkles* suggests a bright light in the distance that gives the illusion of moving a little.
6 Issues concerned with conservation or the environment.
7 You may feel confused, it is not a clear-cut issue, there is no obvious right answer.
8 Something sad or worrying – an illness perhaps or a war.
9 She has said something bad about him that he believes is harming his reputation.
10 It becomes livelier or more interesting.

Unit 44

44.1
1 a **firm/hard** pillow
2 **smooth** skin
3 **tough** lamb chops
4 **blunt** penknife
5 **smooth/calm**
6 **greasy** hair
7 **oily** skin (also **greasy skin**)
8 **bumpy** flight

44.2 *Suggested answers:*

1	Assistant:	Yes. You can either have **matt** or **gloss** (finish).
2	Nelly:	Yes. And the ice on the lake has already **melted**.
3	Bill:	I'm afraid it has **gone hard**.
4	Elana:	Yes, I think attitudes are **hardening / have hardened / are beginning to harden / have begun to harden**.
5	Kate:	Mm. Yes. They are rather old. They're beginning **to go soft**.

44.3

Across	**Down**
3 creamy	1 velvety
4 coarse	2 voices
5 thaw	
6 sticky	

44.4 These are the collocations with the strongest positive or negative associations. You may be able to justify including others in your selection.

positive collocations	**negative collocations**
smooth skin	rough skin
smooth road/flight	greasy hair
tender meat	bumpy road/flight
creamy texture	tough meat
go smoothly	sharp tongue
glossy hair	coarse jokes
	greasy hands
	sticky fingers
	sticky situation

Unit 45

45.1
1 I think caviar must be an acquired taste – I don't like it very much.
2 The delicious aroma of fresh coffee wafted in from the kitchen.
3 The park was spoilt by the noxious fumes from the factory behind it.
4 We just loved the fragrant perfume of the blossom on the trees.
5 I particularly enjoy the subtle flavours that herbs give to food.
6 Smell the bottle and tell me if the milk is sour or OK to drink still.
7 I usually love coffee but this coffee is just too bitter for my taste.
8 It must be the wet logs causing such acrid smoke from the bonfire.

45.2

positive	**negative**
appetising aroma	acrid smoke
fragrant perfume	foul-smelling chemicals
fresh scent	noxious fumes
	overpowering stink
	revolting stench

45.3
1 probably a lot, or at least as much as he can
2 a light smell
a pleasant smell
3 the smell of sweat
4 Just a little – probably to check that it is all right and doesn't, for example, need more salt.
5 No, not at all.
It would have seemed even worse.
6 get the general idea
7 something that has happened
8 They both like a variety of things (e.g. books, films, music, clothes, holidays), not just food.

Unit 46

46.1 1 **a tiny/minute** amount
2 **an enormous** amount
3 **a significant** number
4 **a surprising** number
5 **a considerable/substantial** number

46.2 1 odd
2 currency
3 even
4 comes
5 falling

46.3 1 widespread
2 drop/fall/decline
3 rise
4 rare
5 widespread
6 keep
7 keep
8 rise
9 rare
10 widespread
11 decline/fall
12 rise

46.4 *Possible answers:*
Sales rose steadily/gradually between January and April.
Sales rose sharply/steeply in May.
Sales remained constant between May and August.
Sales fell sharply/steeply in September. / In September there was a dramatic fall in sales.
There was a dramatic rise in sales in November.

Unit 47

47.1 1 quick
2 hasty
3 prompt
4 swift
5 rapid
6 fast
7 brisk
8 speedy

47.2 1 picked
2 moving
3 standstill
4 make/take
5 painfully
6 leisurely
7 took
8 lost
9 lost
10 took

47.3 1 … the **fast** train …
2 … to **steer** the conversation …
3 … **turn** the clock upside down …
4 … in slow **motion**.
5 … **go** astray.
6 … a **quick** lunch …
7 … in **an unhurried** manner.
8 … at **breakneck** speed …
9 … a **top** speed of …

Unit 48

48.1 1 made
2 break
3 habit
4 made
5 slight
6 way
7 adopt

48.2 1 … change the subject.
2 … to change places/seats?
3 … changed my mind. …
4 … changing jobs?
5 … change our clothes …
6 … change the beds.

48.3 1 risen
2 exchanged
3 moving
4 become
5 raise
6 became; arose

Unit 49

49.1
1 ... make a speech.
2 ... gave me her word ...
3 ... get to the point.
4 I wish you luck ...
5 ... cracking/telling jokes.

49.2
1 You can borrow my camera – I'll **give** you instructions about how to use it.
2 I could **tell** you a lot of stories about what we used to do when we were kids.
3 That's enough about computers. I think it's time we **changed** the subject, don't you?
4 On the train I **struck** up a conversation with an interesting man from Japan.
5 I can't **speak** Japanese.
6 I'm afraid I really don't have time for a **lengthy** discussion on the matter.
7 The US President George Washington is famous for confessing after **telling** a lie.
8 I don't like your **tone** of voice – there's no need to be so aggressive.

49.3
1 chat
2 quick
3 ask
4 delicate
5 record
6 make
7 having

49.4
1 ... the truth.
2 ... the subject.
3 ... enough hints.
4 ... observations.
5 ... ignorance.
6 ... the conversation.
7 ... profusely.
8 ... bitterly.
9 ... politely.
10 ... softly.
11 ... in the conversation.
12 ... conversation.

Unit 50

50.1
1 going; take; took
2 pacing; go
3 on foot; go; brisk; go for

50.2
1 False – *Cautiously* means slowly and with great care.
2 False – A leisurely stroll is a slow, relaxed walk.
3 True
4 True
5 False – *Briskly* means quite quickly.

50.3
1 run into / run up against
2 great strides
3 walked it
4 walks of life
5 rush headlong
6 an easy walk

50.4 *Possible collocations include:*
go for a run
break into a run [suddenly start running]
make a run for [escape]
run blindly
run headlong
run a business
(businesses) run efficiently
(things) run smoothly
(buses, trains) run regularly

Unit 51

51.1
1 an early start
2 a promising start
3 a perfect end
4 got off to a good start

51.2 1 It was such a **close** finish to the race that no one was quite sure who had won.
2 I've just got to put the **finishing** touches to my painting and then you can see it.
3 I expect the meeting will **come** to an end at about 5.30. (**draw to a close** is also possible)
4 Everyone is here, so I think we should **make** a start now.
5 We all hope that the negotiations will succeed in **bringing** the strike to an end.
6 E-mail marked the **beginning** of the end for the fax machine.
7 Our journey **ended** – as it had begun – in Cairo.
8 Have you heard yet what the **end** result of the talks was?

51.3 1 I hope the meeting will soon draw to a close.
2 The conference got off to a good start with an excellent reception in the Town Hall.
3 As Dan didn't know a single word of Japanese he was put in an absolute beginners' class.
4 The scandal brought an abrupt end to Jackson's career as a politician. *or* The scandal brought Jackson's career as a politician to an abrupt end.
5 Lance Armstrong won the cycle race in a nail-biting finish.

51.4 1 c 2 d 3 e 4 b 5 f 6 a

Unit 52

52.1

1 won	7 crowning	13 made
2 fruits	8 brings	14 effective
3 brilliant/great	9 made	15 have
4 made	10 guaranteed	16 grasp
5 passed	11 remarkable	17 come
6 gained	12 take	18 dramatic

52.2 1 Our plans went badly wrong.
2 My hopes were dashed when I heard the news.
3 After the horse threw me I lost my nerve and couldn't get back on.
4 The scheme is doomed to failure.
5 He failed his final exams.
6 Our political campaign failed miserably.
7 His plans are a recipe for disaster.
8 A year later he went out of business.
9 She seemed to miss the point completely.
10 His latest novel was a complete flop.

52.3 I was always a dismal **failure** at school. I completely **missed** the point of maths and I failed **miserably** at most other subjects. Only the drama teacher managed to bring **out** the best in me and gave me a part in the school play. However, I lost my **nerve** on the day of the performance and my hopes of a career on the stage were **dashed**.

Unit 53

53.1

1 attracted	4 brought about
2 caused	5 sparked off
3 produce	

53.2

1 sensation	6 positive
2 major	7 affected
3 uproar	8 caused
4 consequences	9 had
5 unexpected	

53.3 1 The enquiry aims to establish what the immediate cause of the fire was.
2 Henry's grandmother had a considerable influence on his choice of career.
3 The changes had some unforeseen results which no one could have predicted.
4 Criticising your previous boss doesn't create a good impression at a job interview.
5 We must do all we can to minimise the impact of the tragedy on our children.
6 What happens in childhood affects the development of personality very deeply.
7 Management is trying to effect some changes in the way the college is structured.
8 The TV coverage they have received has strengthened the impact of the new measures.
9 The government should do something about the underlying causes of crime.
10 The riots were an inevitable result of the huge tax rises.

Follow up

Possible collocations are:

influence – to exert an influence, a considerable influence, a slight influence, a strong influence

effect – to assess the effect, the main effect, short-term/long-term effects

impact – to exaggerate the impact, fundamental impact, international impact

consequences – accept/take the consequences, adverse consequences, likely consequences

There are, however, many other good collocations for these words that you might find.

Unit 54

54.1 1 Well, my **earliest** memory is of sitting in our garden on my mother's lap. I **vaguely** remember that there was a cat or dog there too, but I can't remember much else.
2 I used to have a **good** memory when I was young, but I'm 82 now, and as you get older your **long-term** memory is very clear, but your **short-term** memory is less good. Sometimes I can't remember what happened yesterday. But I can **distinctly/vividly** remember my first day at school as a child.
3 My mother sometimes tells me things I did or said when I was little but which I've **completely/clean** forgotten. One embarrassing memory which I'd rather **blot** out is when I took some scissors and cut my own hair. It looked awful!
4 Seeing schoolchildren often **stirs** up all kinds of memories for me. I wasn't happy at school and I have some **painful** memories of being forced to do sports, which I hated. Sometimes, when I hear certain songs, memories come **flooding** back.

54.2 1 blank 3 clue
2 rightly 4 a memorable / an unforgettable

54.3 1 impression 5 numb
2 sensed 6 sensitive
3 intuition 7 acute
4 over-sensitive 8 sensible

54.4 1 distinctly 4 trust
2 had 5 blot out
3 go

Unit 55

55.1

be	in agreement
come	to a compromise
see	someone's point
settle	our differences
share	an opinion
enter	into an argument
agree	to differ
appreciate	others' points of view

55.2

reaching agreement	*disagreeing*
come to a compromise settle a dispute	a controversy rages a head-on clash a heated argument differences exist

55.3

1 I (can) agree with what you say up to a point.
2 I entirely agree with you.
3 The committee members reached a unanimous agreement.
4 Differences (of opinion) will always arise even between friends.
5 James and Brian strongly disagreed over the question of climate change.
6 The project has been delayed because of a conflict of opinion / because of conflicting opinions among the members of the committee.
7 I find it difficult to go along with such an idea.
8 We fundamentally disagree / disagree fundamentally about most things.

55.4

1 a heated argument
2 a head-on clash, a conflict of opinion
3 controversy rages
4 Because *bitter* usually refers to an unpleasant taste and for most people disagreements are unpleasant and can even be said to leave an unpleasant taste in your mouth.
5 see someone's point

Unit 56

56.1

1 share
2 matter
3 reason
4 belief
5 difference
6 poles
7 firmly
8 believer
9 sneaking

56.2

I **hope** we can / I **wish** we **could** solve a big problem we have regarding our student committee. Opinions are **divided** about how to approach the issue and, naturally, some members have very **strong** opinions. Some of their views are based on their **unshakeable** belief that they are always right and that no one can challenge their **set** of beliefs. My own **considered** opinion is that we should have new elections, but I know that others have quite a different **opinion**.

56.3

	verb	*noun*
1	make	assumptions
2	colour	somebody's judgement
3	trust	
4	attach	importance to
5	cast	doubt on
6	have	serious misgivings doubts

Possible sentences:
1 It is wrong to make assumptions about people before you really get to know them.
2 Recent events have coloured his judgement and he cannot see things objectively any more.
3 I would never trust the judgement of someone who had no experience of the matter.
4 I don't attach much importance to her comments; she knows nothing about the subject.
5 The new statistics cast doubt on the claim that using mobile phones does not damage children's health.
6 I have serious misgivings about the new scheme. I don't think it will work.
Professor Wiseman has doubts about the accuracy of the results of Professor Dumbssort's experiment.

56.4 poles apart
sneaking suspicion
strong opinions
popular belief
cast doubt
firmly believe
think hard

Unit 57

57.1
1 B: Yes, you can't go on putting **off** (**making**) the decision for ever.
2 B: Yes, I'm glad it was a **unanimous** decision.
3 B: Yes, I think it's best if we all **reserve** judgement till we see the results.
4 B: Mm, it's obvious you're having **second** thoughts.
5 B: Yes, I definitely detected a **slight** hesitation on his part, you're right.

57.2

1 sound	3 weigh	5 degree	7 tough	9 give
2 wise	4 arrive	6 defend	8 take	10 come

57.3 1 Archie 2 Elaine 3 Rhoda 4 Mabel 5 Zubaya 6 Kim

Unit 58

58.1
1 leaked document
2 long-running battle
3 heavy/broad hints
4 issue a statement
5 serious allegations
6 clearly implied / dropped heavy/broad hints as to

58.2 1 forward 2 rejects 3 makes 4 acknowledged 5 back 6 substantiate

58.3 1 denied 2 refuse 3 rejects 4 denied 5 refuse

58.4
1 We disclaim responsibility for valuables that are not left in the hotel safe.
2 The pop star insisted that the claims made against him were unfounded.
3 Jones's views run contrary to the facts.
4 The newspaper dropped (heavy/broad) hints about / as to who the actor's new lover was.
5 Paul denied the rumours about him.
6 Whatever idea I suggest, Jim rejects it. *Or* Jim rejects whatever idea I suggest.
7 I don't know what to do, as everyone keeps giving me contradictory advice.
8 The student is facing accusations of cheating in his exam.
9 In his new book the writer puts forward an interesting theory of art.
10 Recent research backs up McIntyre's theory.

Unit 59

59.1
1 In the survey most people expressed a clear/strong preference for coffee rather than tea.
2 Karl has a huge/strong aversion to people using mobile phones in restaurants.
3 The staff all have the highest/greatest regard for their managing director.

4 It's been a great/huge pleasure getting to know you.
5 Suzie has a genuine liking for cowboy films.
6 My parents have a deep/deep-rooted hatred for most modern architecture.
7 We get great enjoyment out of our weekends in the country.
8 Rex took an instant dislike to his new secretary.

59.2 1 – 2 + 3 + 4 – 5 – 6 + 7 – 8 + 9 +

59.3

1 cater	3 particular	5 warm	7 thought
2 strong	4 give	6 take	

59.4 *Possible answers:*

1 I like both, but I suppose it is a fantastice feeling when you give something and you can tell that the person you give it to really likes it.
2 I think I am more likely to take an intense dislike to a person than a place as my feelings in general – both liking and disliking – are stronger for people than places.
3 I normally go for an aisle seat because I like to be able to stretch my legs.
4 I don't have a singer who I could call my absolute favourite – I like a lot of different people, and who I want to listen to depends on my mood.
5 Tony Benn, an elderly British politician, has filled me with admiration over the last five years. I think he is principled and intelligent, which is not something that can be said about all politicians.
6 I take more pride in my work, if, by home, you mean the house that I live in. But if by home you mean family then I take more pride in my home.
7 I feel great love for my husband, my son and my nephews.
8 I personally get more pleasure from reading.

Unit 60

60.1

1 standing	5 richly/justly	9 singing
2 thunderous	6 won	10 justly/richly
3 acclaim	7 take	11 offer
4 warmly	8 gives	12 round

60.2

1 T
2 F – If you have nothing but praise for someone, you praise them a lot and have no criticisms to make of them.
3 F – If you criticise someone roundly, you criticise them very strongly.
4 T
5 F – If you counter criticism, you criticise your critic back.
6 F – If someone gives their blessing to something, they say they are in favour of it.
7 T
8 T

60.3

1 He came in for a lot of criticism.
2 I thoroughly disapprove of how she responded to the criticism.
3 The judge severely condemned him / condemned him severely for lying.
4 I want to express my disapproval of her behaviour.
5 The critics were outspoken but he dismissed their criticisms.
6 His comments received universal condemnation.
7 We strenuously objected to the plan and were highly critical of it.
Or: We were highly critical of the plan and strenuously objected to it.
8 I have always been a harsh critic of corrupt government.

60.4 This is the last exercise in this book. May we give you a pat on the **back** for getting to this point. Indeed, you **richly/justly** deserve a **big** clap. We have **nothing** but praise for you and would like to **offer** you our warm congratulations!

Index